DISCOVER
KAYAK FISHING

Andy Benham

A PRACTICAL MANUAL

First published 2010
Reprinted 2013

Published in Great Britain 2010 by Pesda Press
Unit 22, Galeri
Doc Victoria
Caernarfon
Gwynedd
LL55 1SQ

ISBN: 978–1–906095–22–2

Printed and bound in Poland. www.hussarbooks.pl

Dedicated to Jack and Yiannis,
two people just starting out in
the world. I hope they will be
both better paddlers and better
anglers than I've ever been.

CONTENTS

THE AUTHOR
Andy Benham

Andy has been a sea angler for as long as he can remember, growing up on Brighton beach with a fishing rod in his hands and owning a variety of small boats through his teens.

He became a journalist, working on a number of magazines including *Angling Times*, *Sea Angler*, *Trout & Salmon*, *Boat Angler* and *Improve Your Coarse Fishing*. During his time working on the angling magazines he was able to fish with some of the UK's best anglers, and was lucky enough to fish in some amazing locations, including making a Nile Perch video with TV legend John Wilson. He then moved on to spend a spell at the BBC, and worked for magazines such as *BBC Wildlife* and *Countryfile*.

More recently Andy has quit the rat race and moved to a house overlooking the sea in South Devon, so he can spend more time afloat in his kayak and fishing from the shore. He can also paddle to his favourite pub, on the other side of the estuary. He became *Sea Angler's* regular kayak fishing correspondent in 2009 and has written a series of articles on the subject for the magazine. His latest project is Devonkayakfishing.com

ACKNOWLEDGEMENTS

I wouldn't be doing this if it weren't for some of you out there, so thanks are due to loads of people. I'll start, however, by apologising to anyone I've forgotten as there are bound to be a few. First of all I'd like to thank everyone on the Anglers Afloat website for the amazing amount of help offered. Special thanks go to Eugene for taking me out on my first serious offshore trip, to Adam for babysitting me on more than one occasion, to James for offering encouragement and to Paul for some serious training delivered with a light heart. I'd also like to say a big thank you to Mark Crame, not just for his photography, including the cover shot, but also for all the help and encouragement he's given me, as well as some splendid days out. Elaine Rowan also deserves a mention for knocking the raw copy into shape, and for coming up with some good ideas for the final flow of the chapters. Thanks go to the geographically challenged Nick who shared a lot of my first steps, provided more bait than I dare to remember and has always been an all-round good egg.

Jemma and all the staff at AS Watersports deserve a mention for all the help and encouragement they provided in the early days and for being forward thinking enough to provide free training.

All photos by Andy Benham unless credited.

Thank you to all that have contributed photographs including Ocean Kayak, Wilderness Systems, Palm, Scotty, Werner, Garmin, Icom, Mark Crame, Nick Webb, David Morris and Kate Brown.

Finally, I would like to say a big thank you to Kate for putting up with me disappearing for days on end and typing this book in the only warm room in the house during one of the coldest winters I can remember.

FOREWORD

This book is primarily about sea fishing from a kayak, although it does take a look at some of the other waters you can fish. In the UK and Ireland the coast is never far away.

This book is not a compendium of knots, rigs and the craft of fishing. If you're new to fishing I'd recommend *The Sea Angler's Guide to Bait and Rigs*, edited by Mel Russ – very good step by step stuff.

Kayak angling is booming as more and more people take up the sport. A kayak is relatively cheap, completely transportable, and provides you with access to deep water fishing, previously the domain of boat owners or those prepared to go charter fishing. You even get a boat all to yourself.

It's not just the great fishing which is attractive - many are drawn by the activity itself. Anglers turn to kayaking to up their catch rates, but get hooked on the paddling as well as the fishing. It's a great way to get around, fantastic exercise, and immensely sociable. There's a thriving social scene and numerous clubs, meetings and shared fishing trips taking place every year.

You can paddle your kayak in places which can't be reached by larger boats, and your stealthy approach (beyond the reach of engines) lets you slip quietly past timid seals and seabirds . Sitting around, waiting for a fish to bite, surrounded by amazing scenery and wildlife, it's easy to see just why kayak fishing is becoming so popular.

A ROD AND A KAYAK

I started kayaking for one simple reason: I wanted to catch more fish. For years I fished an estuary in North Devon but had been pushed off my favourite sandbank by the rising tides. One day I met a man in the dunes, manhandling a bizarre plastic boat to the water's edge. That was my first contact with a kayak fisherman. He'd only been out a few times and had yet to catch a fish, but it sowed a seed in my mind. The seed sprouted and, a couple of weeks later, I made a few exploratory phone calls.

The river Torridge at Appledore, where I first saw someone fishing from a kayak.

I've tried to write this book in much the same way as I got involved with the sport. I certainly don't claim to be an expert; with around fifty trips under my belt so far I'm definitely still learning and will probably continue to do so for as long as I go kayaking (I've certainly found this to be the case fishing from dry land).

I'll freely admit to being rather nervous about the whole kayaking thing when I started looking at it for the first time. I've been an avid angler all my life and ended up moving down to Devon, as much for the bass fishing as anything else. The place I tended to fish was at the mouth of a river out near the bar. Every summer I'd have at least one close call as the tide came in threatening to cut me off just as the fishing was starting to get interesting. There had to be some way to stay out there longer, but it was very shallow and indeed very tranquil so a boat seemed a little over the top. After my chance encounter in the dunes, however, a kayak seemed like the ideal tool for the job.

9

I browsed the web and uncovered a few kayak fishing websites, most notably Anglers Afloat, and the address of my local water-sports emporium. AS Watersports (a kayak shop in Exeter) was running a kayak fishing day. If they are still doing them and you live down that way, then a trip along is well worth it. I found the kayak fishing fraternity to be a very helpful bunch. Indeed, everyone was very keen for me to try out a kayak there and then. A lack of bottle and no change of clothing meant that I went away filled with ideas but without trying out any of the huge range of kayaks on offer.

The following weekend I was back at the shop and booked onto one of their try-it-out sessions. This involved two hours messing around on the Exeter canal with an instructor and another six kayaking wannabes, aged from 20 to around 60 and all very nervous. I was convinced that I was going to be spending most of the next couple of hours spluttering in the canal, having been evicted from a monumentally unstable kayak. It came as something of a surprise, therefore, to find that not only was it fairly easy to get into (or rather onto) a kayak, but it was actually rather difficult to turn one over. In fact, in the whole two hours when I tried about half a dozen kayaks, I didn't capsize once.

Moreover, within a couple of hours I was hooked on kayaking. I'd only decided to get a kayak to enhance my fishing, so was very surprised to find that I'd become completely hooked on a different

sport within just a couple of hours. Gliding down the canal using your own strength for propulsion was simply magical. The swans came over to say hello, I passed a family of ducks complete with a dozen ducklings in line astern of the proud parents and mystery fish came up from the depths to create slowly dissipating swirls on the surface. It was amazing.

It took ages for the grin to leave my face, but only a matter of hours for me to find a local kayaking coach and book my first training session. Getting a few lessons from a professional coach under your belt is a really good way to start. My coach also introduced me to the joys of falling in. Although the Exeter canal in May isn't the warmest place to practise your re-entry skills, it's amazing how falling in (and getting back on) a few times will boost your confidence.

In the first chapter 'Getting Started' I look at how to make that step from an angler to a kayak angler. I had thought about buying a kayak for ages before I took the plunge, so to speak. It really pays to carry out as much internet research as possible before you buy your first kayak. When I started out, I registered on a number of forums and spent around four months lurking in the darker corners. I tried to figure out what people were talking about, what type of kayak I should be looking for, where to buy it from and what kind of gear I'd need.

One of the first questions that you'll probably want answered is how much is it all going to cost? A decent sit-on-top kayak, brand new, will probably run to around £700 or so. You can buy them second-hand on eBay, but they do tend to hold their value remarkably well so don't expect any bargains. Sometimes you can pick up a kayak already fitted out for angling from someone who is upgrading to a different boat.

After having shelled out the money on the kayak, you're only at the start of the process. I did a rough running total of what my kayak has cost so far and the answer is just over a couple of grand – that doesn't include the fishing gear!

As well as the kayak itself you're going to need a paddle, and you'll find that spending a little more on a decent paddle is a really good investment. The right clothing for the conditions in which you are going to fish 'What to Wear' (p28) and a decent amount of safety kit 'Safety Kit' (p36) are also important. On top of that you'll be looking at some fitting-out for the kayak 'Fitting Out your Kayak' (p46) and a decent training course to set you off in the right direction 'Kayaking with Confidence' (p56). Last but certainly not least, you should acquire some knowledge about the environment into which you are heading 'Seamanship for Kayak Anglers' (p64).

After setting yourself up, various gadgets are available to enhance your kayak fishing experience. Although a GPS 'Using GPS to Navigate' (p72) shouldn't be considered as a substitute for a compass, it can be a useful addition to your safety kit. A fish finder 'See Underwater with a Fishfinder' (p76) can help to guide you to the most successful marks and a VHF radio 'Handheld VHF Radios at Sea' (p86) will let you keep in touch with your fishing buddies when out on the water and, more importantly, with the coastguard. These gadgets highlight where kayaking and kayak fishing diverge. Kayaking is often portrayed as one man and his boat, and you'll find a very purist attitude at some kayaking stores when you ask for bits to stick onto your kayak.

We finally get around to the fish in 'Fishing Skills' (p92). Tips on technique and what to fish for are covered in 'What to Fish for' (p105). I caught my first fish on my first trip out. I can still remember every detail of it: a small school bass of around 2lb took a liking to a Yo Zori lure on just my third cast at my favourite fishing spot. Again, the grin took weeks to disappear. Combining fishing with kayaking was as close to nirvana as I was ever likely to get.

I've really come to appreciate the kayaking side of things. I'll even go out of an evening and have a paddle along the Devon coastline without a rod, just to soak up some scenery. Kayaking has opened up a whole new way of seeing the coast; some places I thought I knew well have presented a whole new side to themselves when seen from the seat of a kayak.

Andy on the river trolling for bass at the start of his kayak fishing adventure. Photo: Nick Webb.

As one of the UK's fastest growing sports, kayak fishing is also a very new sport for which the rules have still to be written 'Taking it Further' (p129). When I started I couldn't find a good book on the subject – there are loads on kayaking but none of them covered everything I wanted to know. I have a lot of people to thank for their help in putting this together. The kayak fishing fraternity are a very friendly bunch, and loads of people have freely chipped in with help and advice.

I hope that I can impart some of fun I've had and some of the lessons I've learnt (from my mistakes). I hope that you learn something from the book and enjoy your own experiences as much as I've enjoyed mine. I'm still very proud to count myself as a beginner, and admit that I learn something new every time afloat.

When you go out kayak fishing please be aware that you are taking a risk. I treat my kayak like I treat my chainsaw: it's a handy tool which I love to use. Both require proper training and safety equipment and both are capable of killing you if you are careless. Kayak fishing is not about demonstrating bravado. Take it easy, always paddle within your limits and don't be afraid of walking away from a launch if you think the conditions are beyond your experience. Enjoy your time afloat, but stay safe.

GETTING STARTED

Photo: David Morris

AnglersAfloat.co.uk

For the purposes of this book I'm going to assume that you are intending to fish from a sit-on-top (SOT) kayak rather than the more traditional sit-in kayak (SINK). It was really the start of sit-on-top kayaks that heralded the advent of kayak fishing as we know it today. They can carry all the requisite gear, are easy to get back on top of if you fall in and, if you go for a plastic one, are fairly cheap to buy.

The modern fishing kayak's relative cheapness is partly due to the mode of production: rotomoulding. Plastic is put into a mould which is then spun to thinly coat the inside. Any necessary attachment points can be easily incorporated. The finished kayak comes out of the mould in a single piece, without the join between top and bottom mouldings common on more traditional designs.

Fishing kayaks come in all shapes, colours and sizes.

Try before you buy

This may be stating the obvious, but you should always try to have a play with at least two or three kayaks before parting with your hard-earned cash. It can be difficult to make the right decision however, particularly if you haven't been on a sit-on-top before. When I started kayaking I lacked confidence and expected to capsize at any moment. I rated kayaks by how wide they were as, everything else being equal, a wider kayak is more stable at rest on flat water. This was a bit of a mistake; as my kayaking improved I found that very stable kayaks were also slow and difficult to paddle. There are many compromises to kayak design.

Longer kayaks are nearly always faster than shorter kayaks. The converse is that longer kayaks are harder to turn and less manoeuvrable. If you want to play in the surf you will find that dedicated surfing kayaks are very short indeed (not much more than 2m long), while a serious offshore touring kayak can be 5m or more in length.

The first thing to consider when setting out to buy a kayak is where you want to fish. If the answer is close to the shore or in estuaries then a kayak of around 3.5–4m might be a good choice. You'll own a lighter and more manoeuvrable boat and will also save a bit of money. The only downside to this approach is that kayak fishing can be addictive; I've lost count of the number of people who decide just to go out a few hundred metres but end up heading offshore to wrecks and going out in all weathers. It might be worth getting something just a little bigger so that, if you do decide to take your fishing a bit further, then your kayak is up to the job.

Choosing just one kayak to do all your fishing is quite difficult. I know of people who have given up trying to find their ideal kayak and have bought two: a shorter, lighter boat for inshore fun and a longer kayak for serious offshore paddling.

Plastic kayaks come in an amazing range of colours but for sea fishing I'd stick to one of the brighter colours, e.g. red, yellow or orange. At sea I always want to be seen from as far away as possible and I'd be a bit wary about paddling in a green or blue kayak.

The next question is who is going to go fishing? If there are two of you, or if you intend to try fishing with your kids, then you might want to look at a double kayak. Ocean Kayak's Malibu 2XL is a popular choice (it's the boat that is often for hire at surf beaches and canal sides), which can be outfitted for kayak fishing. It can carry two adults with a small child, so it's a good family boat. The Wilderness Systems Tarpon 130T is another decent double kayak without the third seat.

Capable of taking a third small passenger in the middle, the 2XL is a very popular tandem. Photo: oceankayak.com

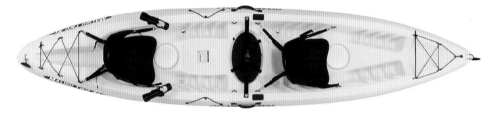

The problem with double kayaks is that they are quite heavy and can be difficult to paddle with just a single person; the majority of fishing kayaks sold are therefore single-seaters.

For me, comfort comes very high up on my list of requirements when choosing a kayak. Comfort is personal; a kayak seat that is like a armchair for one person will be torture for another, so it pays to sit in as many kayaks as possible before forking out. Even if you don't like the seat that comes with the kayak (and the manufacturer doesn't offer an upgrade), then you may be able to buy a third party seat. Look for an adjustable seat which gives some support to the lower back.

The seat can make an amazing difference to the comfort of your kayak, for better or worse.

The size of the paddler is also another factor to take into consideration when choosing a kayak. Firstly, there is the weight that you are asking the kayak to support. If you are of larger-than-average build, make sure that you buy a kayak that will take not just you but also all the gear you might wish to carry. The other factor is the width of your rear end and the length of your legs, both of which can be an issue with some designs, so try out a number of kayaks.

Once you've got the seat sorted and know the kayak will take your weight, have a look at the cockpit and, in particular, the position of the footpegs. Are they adjustable and, if so, can you reach forward easily to adjust them? When paddling you want your knees slightly bent, so see if you can get the pegs in the right place. This is largely a matter of how tall you are and some kayaks just don't work for either smaller or taller paddlers. It's also worth thinking about where you will be mounting rod rests and fish finders and the like. Does the cockpit layout allow you to reach the mounting positions easily, and can you twist round to reach the rear tank well behind you? These are questions that only you will be able to answer after spending a bit of time in the kayak.

Trying out a kayak with full fishing kit is where a fishing kayak meet or demo day really helps. You'll find out things about the kayaks which won't be obvious from a catalogue or at a shop showroom.

Something else worth thinking about is storage. Kayaks come with a bewildering range of hatches – some have long rod pods which take up the space between your legs but let you get your rods safely inside the hull if you are likely to be launching or retrieving in surf. Another factor is the hatches themselves which range from quite complicated with waterproof locking mechanisms to simple covers held in place with straps.

All these add-ons increase the weight of the kayak. You may occasionally have to carry your kayak to the sea single-handed, or if you drive a four-by-four or van then you may have to lift your kayak over your head to put it on a roof rack. Think carefully before buying one of the heavier designs as you may end up having to ask for help to get it on top of your transport. If possible, try lifting the kayak yourself with rod rests and other accessories installed rather than relying on the manufacturers statistics.

Lifting and moving a kayak

If you are going to hurt your back kayaking, the chances are it will be lifting your kayak rather than on the water. Plastic kayaks are pretty indestructible and can be dragged, although you will wear out the bottom eventually.

- Use a trolley wherever possible.

- Fishing with a friend is not only safer, but gives you someone to help load the kayak.

- Don't pile all the gear into the kayak at the side of your car if you then have to carry the kayak to the water; make multiple trips with smaller loads.

- Always use your legs to do the lifting and keep your back straight (think of all those health and safety videos!)

- Check your route to the sea and make sure it's not too slippery or rocky. It's easy to trip or sprain an ankle on an unseen rock or slip on a muddy slipway.

- Use the moulded-in straps or toggles and carry points to lift the kayak; they are well anchored and spread the load.

Makes and models

When it comes to individual kayaks, it's impossible to offer a recommendation without knowing something about you and where you are going to fish. If pressed for a shortlist, however, I would recommend that you try out one of the following kayaks.

Tarpon 140
by Wilderness Systems

Length 4.3m | Width 71cm | Weight 32kg | Capacity 170kg

The Tarpon 140 and the smaller 120 are beautifully built boats, but are slightly heavier than the rest. Channels down the bottom of the hull mean it tracks very well and is at home in snotty seas, but it can be more difficult to turn as a result and is a little slower than other boats. The seat is, in my opinion, the best on the market. The finish is excellent.

Scupper Pro
by Ocean Kayak

Length 4.5m | Width 66cm | Weight 25kg | Capacity 160–180kg

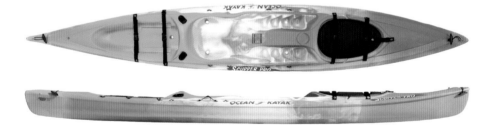

This is probably the fastest of the plastic kayaks, but as the seat is so low it can be a wet ride. The seat is also relatively narrow, so make sure you can fit into it. The Scupper Pro is very good for rougher conditions and for longer distance paddles, and, unusually for a fishing SOT, it can even surf.

Prowler Elite 4.5

Length 4.5m | Width 71cm | Weight 30.4kg | Capacity 230kg

If pressed, I would probably say the Prowler Elite is Ocean Kayak's best all-rounder. It is fast and stable and has a decent amount of storage space. It has an uncluttered cockpit arrangement that some people will find appealing, but also has plenty of space for fitting rod rests, fish finders and the like.

Prowler Trident 13 Angler

Length 4.1m | Width 74.9cm | Weight 27.2kg | Capacity 193–216kg

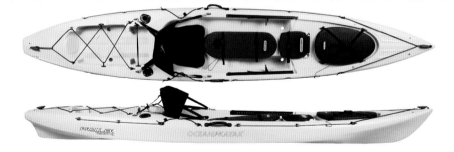

The Prowler 13 Angler and its bigger brother, the Prowler 15, are probably the best equipped of all fishing kayaks. They have a rod pod to take all your gear and specially modified scupper holes and mountings for fitting a fish finder. The extra volume up front also enables them to ride over the waves rather than pushing through them.

Prowler Ultra 4.7
by Ocean Kayak

Length 4.7m | Width 74cm | Weight 35kg (without rudder) | Capacity 180kg

The new boy on the block, and if you want all the whistles and bells, then this is the yak for you. The down sides are the price and the weight, but the plus sides are amazing. It's very fast, dry and stable, has a revolving rod pod top to hide your fish finder during surf landings, more fixing points than any other kayak, live bait tank, wear strip on the hull and more.

Dorado
by Kaskazi

Length 4.8m | Width 63cm | Weight 26kg | Capacity 180kg

The Dorado is the only glass fibre kayak on the list. It's the top of the range in sit-on-tops and is very fast and stable. They are more costly but slightly less robust than a plastic kayak. The glass fibre construction makes lifting this yak a doddle, and fitting transducers for a fish finder is also exceptionally easy, although it also one of the most expensive yaks here.

Choosing a paddle

Your choice of paddle is just as important as your choice of kayak (in some ways even more so). You are going to have to lift your paddle for every stroke you make, and you're going to be in intimate contact with it for every second that you are moving.

Paddle choice starts by choosing the right type of blade for the type of paddling that you are going to be doing. In kayaking terms (at least for paddle selection), kayak fishing is classed as touring. A touring paddle tends to have longer, thinner, asymmetric blades and tends to weigh less and be of a lighter construction than a general paddle or a whitewater paddle.

Asymmetric blades have less area below the shaft, but have to be used the right way up. Their design enables the two sides of the blade to exert an even pressure on the shaft, which prevents the paddle shaft from trying to turn in the paddler's hands. In extreme cases, a big turning moment on the shaft can lead to injury. (One of my instructors has an impressive picture of himself flying over a particularly nasty looking waterfall. He claims the photo is ruined by the fact that he is holding his paddle the wrong way up, wrecking his credibility.)

My Werner paddle has asymmetric blades, where the top and bottom edges of the blade are different lengths.

The weight of the paddle you are going to use is a really crucial consideration. The first paddle I was given at a demo session weighed next to nothing as it was made from carbon fibre. When I bought my kayak I asked how much the paddle cost, expecting to have to pay around £40. I was shocked to be told that my demo paddle cost no less than £200.

It was only when I went out with a bog-standard £40 paddle that I learnt to appreciate the difference between the two. Paddling with a lightweight paddle is an absolute pleasure, and I'm really glad that the shop talked me into buying the more expensive paddle in the first place. A lot of the people I fish with bought a cheap paddle to start with and then upgraded within a few months, often after borrowing a friend's more expensive paddle.

Most people go for a two-piece paddle, which helps a lot when it comes to fitting the paddle into your car. Some paddles also have the option of rotating the blades to different angles, known as feathering. Choosing the right feather will make paddling easier on your wrists. Again, feather is a personal thing; try out a number of different settings to see what suits you best.

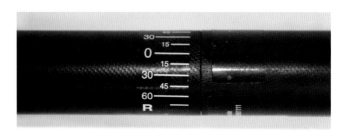

The two-piece shaft on this paddle allows the angle of the blades to be changed to suit you.

The length of your paddle is another area where it's difficult to give a definitive answer. Paddle length is governed by two factors: the height of the paddler and the width of the kayak. A standard test is to stand with your arm extended upward. The distance from your fingertips to the ground is a rough indication of the paddle length you need. This method has been around for ages and assumes that all kayaks are the same width. For a wider boat, you'll need a longer paddle to comfortably reach the water on either side.

Paddle length (in cm from the tip to tip of each blade) depends on the width of the kayak, as well as on the height of the paddler.
Image: Werner Paddles

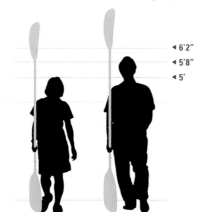

◄ 6'2"
◄ 5'8"
◄ 5'

LOW ANGLE PADDLERS

BOAT WIDTH

HEIGHT	UNDER 58cm	58–71cm	OVER 71cm
UNDER 5'	210	220	230
5'–5'6"	215	220	230
5'6"–6"	220	220	230
OVER 6'	220	230	240

HIGH ANGLE PADDLERS

BOAT WIDTH

HEIGHT	UNDER 66cm	OVER 66cm
UNDER 5'4"	205	210
5'4"–6'	210	215
OVER 6'	215	220

Try before you buy – find a good dealer and try a number of different paddles until you find one that feels right. If the point where the blade joins the shaft is well under water while paddling, then the paddle is probably too long. If you find it difficult to get the blade fully under water, then it's probably too short.

Alternative propulsion

But do you actually need a paddle? There are other ways of propelling a kayak, pedal power and even electric motors. The Hobie Mirage uses pedals to drive a set of flippers below the waterline and is capable of some considerable speed. I remember the first time I saw one coming at me across Poole harbour: the 'paddler' was sitting back with his hands behind his head, whistling happily as the kayak sped along.

Although it divides opinion, I'm a big fan of the battery-powered Torque.

It is difficult to know where to draw the line as Hobie's Adventure model can even be fitted with a sail and dagger board. Is this really a kayak? At the end of the day, this type of craft can be great fun and having your hands free can really make fishing easy (particularly when you are trolling lures).

For the ultimate hands-free craft then look no further than Ocean Kayak's Torque, another design which divides the kayaking world. I love the idea of a removable electric motor (which runs off a car battery) providing a speed of around 5 knots and power to run all day. Others, however, will turn up their nose and cry 'foul'.

Kayak transport

It's also a good idea to think about getting your brand-new kayak to the water. Most people will choose to strap their kayak to their car roofrack. It's probably best to avoid ratchet-type straps as these can be over-tightened and may deform the hull in the process. Most watersports dealers sell cam straps with buckles that are attached to a flap of neoprene. Not only are they harder to over-tighten, but the neoprene flap also protects the plastic hull from the metal buckle.

Providing you've chosen a kayak which you can easily lift on your own, getting it off the car shouldn't be a problem. Getting it to the water's edge usually involves using a trolley of some kind. C-Tug has a massive share of the kayak trolley market, to the point that it's unusual to see anything else on the beach. These neat little plastic trolleys come with pneumatic tyres and easily break down into a number of pieces, all of which are small enough to pass through the front hatch of just about every kayak on the market.

The C-Tug helps you to lug your kayak over even the roughest ground.

C-Tugs are rather like Marmite in that you either love them or hate them. I've seen wars break out on websites over its design. I'm rather at a loss as to why this happens, as I thoroughly recommend them. Make sure you do up the buckle as shown in the instructions, and you should never have a problem.

If you fancy standing out from the crowds then you can make your own or buy another type (e.g. Eckla), a small number of which are available from kayak shops.

A trolley takes the strain out of moving your kayak..

WHAT TO WEAR

When you first start out kayak fishing you might see people out and about in just swimwear with perhaps a T-shirt. There's nothing wrong with this at the height of summer or – even better – when fishing overseas in more temperate climates. However, it can become cold very quickly in the UK. Being out on the water and frequently quite damp (if not wet), kayaking does require you to dress appropriately for the weather conditions you are likely to encounter. More importantly, you should dress for the water temperature that you are likely to encounter if you end up swimming. When the water is still quite warm during autumn, I often fish in a wetsuit. Even on a nice warm day during spring, however, I wear a dry suit because the water temperature is still very low.

Wetsuits

The next step up from swimwear is to invest in a wetsuit. There is a huge choice out there and a surfing wetsuit can be picked up for an amazingly low price.

Make sure that your arms have free movement for paddling. Some surfers' wetsuits are quite restrictive across the shoulders;

sleeveless wetsuits are often much better for paddling. The length of leg is down to personal choice but a sleeveless, long-legged wetsuit will often fit the bill.

The other thing to think about is the position of the zip. Surfing wetsuits are designed for a wearer who is going to be lying down on their front or standing up. In a kayak, however, you will spend nearly all your time sitting down and therefore want the zip to be at the front rather than the back. Many of the major brands sell wetsuits that are suitable for kayaking. For summer, 3mm neoprene thickness is alright but wetsuits are really a summer only item. If you want to fish later on in the year, then you are going to have to look at something else.

Paddle pants and cags

The next step up from wearing a wetsuit is to invest in some clothing that, rather than just keeping you warm when you are wet, will keep you dry in the first place. There are two options: an all-in-one dry suit or a combination of waterproof top (more commonly known as a cag) and waterproof trousers (also known as paddle pants).

Because fishing from a sit-on-top is a relatively new activity, there isn't a huge amount of specially designed kit out there. Most cags and paddle pants on the market are designed for use with a sit-in kayak. As a result, the tops can be very waterproof indeed but the pants are designed for someone spending their time inside a boat rather than on top of it. An additional problem with this type of clothing is the seal between the top and trousers; it can be difficult to get a waterproof seal between the top and bottom half.

Paddle pants come in two varieties: those that have a built-in waterproof sock which keep your feet dry and those that finish at the ankle. The pants without feet are more flexible (you can

On the sea I'd really recommend a hat with a brim or a baseball cap. They keep the saltwater out of your eyes (concentrated salt solution collects in your eyebrows, not nice). A hat may also provide some sun and eye protection whilst fishing. Photo: emotionkayaks.com

slip them on and off easily as conditions change) and work well in warmer weather, but the ankle seal may let some water in.

A standalone dry top can be worn with a wetsuit, paddle pants or shorts. It is a very useful outer shell for layering your clothing and can be packed away small for when a summer day turns breezy. This one has latex neck and wrist seals with neoprene over-cuffs. Photo: palmequipmenteurope.com

I tend to think of a cag and paddle pants as useful pieces of kit for the late spring and autumn, when the flexibility of a two-piece can come in very handy. When it starts to get colder, however, then the one-piece dry suit comes into its own.

Dry suits

A dry suit does exactly what it says on the tin. The better models are also breathable so stop you becoming too hot, a major factor if you are planning on doing a lot of paddling to get to your fishing spot. You get into the suit by means of a watertight zip, which either runs across the chest or across the shoulders. I use a front-entry suit, which I find easier to get in and out of on those times that I fish on my own. Other anglers swear by back-entry suits, however, as the zip across your chest is somewhat inflexible and can make it more difficult to paddle.

Looking after the zip is crucial to keeping the suit in good condition. You can either use a stick of beeswax to keep it running smoothly, or buy one of the many proprietary zip lubricants. Make sure that you buy a lubricant which is approved for your suit, as you can inadvertently damage the zip by using the wrong type.

A stick of beeswax is the best lubrication for the zip of your dry suit.

Apart from the zip, the other main dry suit features to consider are the seals at the neck and the wrists. These will nearly always be either latex or neoprene. Latex provides a better seal against the skin, but can be more uncomfortable to wear for long periods. Most suits have a series of rings marked on the seals, and the user then cuts back the seal to the appropriate ring to get a good fit. If a suit feels like it is cutting off all the blood to your head, it probably means you should cut back the seals a little further.

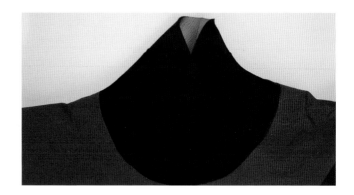

A vital point to think about when buying a dry suit is how you can relieve yourself. Once the fishing bug has bitten you can end up spending many hours afloat, often a long way out at sea. Being desperate to go to the loo in a suit with no easy means of doing so is not one of life's great pleasures. Some suits have a separate relief zip built in and others can have them fitted. I very strenuously recommend that you consider this when buying your suit!

You will be able to fish all year round with a dry suit, but you will also have to wear a number of layers under the suit as they don't provide much warmth. As a rule-of-thumb, dress for the conditions and then put the dry suit on over the top. The same rules apply to dressing under a dry suit as for general outdoor wear: use a series of layers starting with a base layer to wick moisture away from your skin and then a middle and an outer layer. Some dry suits come complete with a fleece under-suit, so it's worth shopping around for the best deal.

Boots

It's also worth spending some money to keep your extremities warm as both the hands and feet can get very cold in the winter. Even in the summer, it's worth having something on your feet to protect them from cuts and scrapes.

For warm-water paddling I use a pair of water shoes. These are like trainers but with far better drainage so that the water just runs out. If the water is a little cold, then this kind of shoe can be worn with thin neoprene socks to provide a little more insulation. Crocs are also good if all you want to do is protect your feet.

The next stage up is to wear diver's wetsuit boots. These can be very effective as they trap a layer of water inside the boot and then use your body heat to warm it up (like a wetsuit itself). The thicker the neoprene, the warmer and tougher the boot will be.

Dry-suit wearers have two choices: either keep everything dry or go down the same route as described above and use wetsuit boots or a kayaking shoe. Wetsuit boots can be quite effective if you put on a couple of pairs of socks under the dry suit to insulate your toes. The feet of your dry suit will either be made of the same fabric as the dry suit or from latex (the former are generally warmer).

Suits can have latex feet, like this one, or some offer the slightly warmer cloth version.

With either type of foot however, there is still water in contact with the suit if you only wear wetsuit boots. In the depths of winter, you can still get really cold feet. For very cold conditions I wear a pair of knee-high neoprene boots over the top of the dry suit which, providing I don't wade out into the water, keeps the water away from my feet entirely. They are a close fit around the

A good pair of boots will keep your feet dry and warm, even in the depths of winter. Photo: palmequipmenteurope.com

upper calf and form quite a good seal. Even if you end up taking a dip, very little water gets into the boots; if it does, they are made of neoprene and work like wetsuit boots.

With two pairs of skiing socks under a dry suit and neoprene boots on top, you can keep your feet quite toasty. When buying boots it's always best to try them on first, but try them with your dry suit and a couple of pairs of socks (I have size 10 feet, but wear size 12 neoprene boots).

Gloves

What to wear on your hands is probably a little more problematic. I've yet to find a pair of gloves that keep my hands really warm and dry but also let me handle bait and fishing equipment. You can buy neoprene paddling gloves which are quite effective. Fingerless versions are the most dextrous, but tend to be colder than full gloves.

Another way to keep your hands warm in the depths of winter is to carry a chemical gel hand warmer (sold for hiking or climbing). These work out at around £1 a sachet and can give you some degree of warmth for around 6 hours – this can make all the difference on a really long cold session. Rechargeable versions are also available. I tend to keep a pair of the chemical type in my fishing box over the winter, so that I can warm up my hands if necessary.

Gear maintenance

It's important to look after all your gear. Ensure that you rinse everything thoroughly with fresh water after you use it – fishing can be a messy business and an un-rinsed dry suit forgotten in the back of the car can quickly become quite unpleasant. After rinsing, all clothing should be left to dry as naturally as possible. Remember to look after the zip of your dry suit, which should be lubricated after each use and left in the position recommended by the suit manufacturer (usually open).

Dressed for the worst on a breezy but sunny day, comfortable in a drysuit made of breathable fabric. Should the weather turn foul or the day turn out to be a long one, you'll be glad to have remained warm and dry from the start. Photo: Mike Webb.

SAFETY KIT

Photo: wildernesssystems.com

It may come as a surprise to learn that in the UK, unlike other countries, there is no statutory requirement to have any safety kit with you when you venture out on a kayak. However – and this is a big however – this doesn't mean that it is even remotely a good idea not to carry one. You may be tempted to nip out for a quick paddle from your local beach and just catch a few mackerel. However, the sea is fundamentally a dangerous place and conditions can change very rapidly. With kayaking, rather like the Scouts, the motto has to be 'Be Prepared'; that way, should the worst happen, you will be ready for it.

So what exactly should you take with you when you venture out in search of the next big one? When I did my training, there were two items about which my trainer was adamant that you should have with you. He would refuse to go out on the water with you if you lacked either a PFD (personal floatation device) or a paddle leash (to keep your paddle attached to your kayak should you take an unexpected dip).

A fully kitted-out kayak angler, complete with hand-bearing compass and day and night flare.

Personal floatation devices

A PFD is really just a modern take on those cork-filled horseshoe shaped life jackets that have been around since the days of the Titanic. A modern PFD will probably have a little less floatation than a lifejacket and may not turn the wearer face up if they fall in. It will however help you keep afloat, be comfortable to wear and let you paddle (or swim) with ease.

It's important to try on a number of PFDs to make sure you have a really comfortable fit. When fishing you may be sitting still for eight hours or more, so you want something that is really comfortable. Don't just try on the PFD standing up, but make sure it doesn't ride up around the neck when you sit down. Not only must the PFD be comfortable when you are sitting about fishing, it's also got to give you good freedom of movement for your shoulders so it doesn't interfere with your paddling.

Riding up can be a problem with PFDs, and you may notice this when you are practicing recoveries. This usually means that either the PFD is a bad fit or, more commonly, that not all the straps are done up. It can be tempting to just zip up a PFD and not fasten all the straps. This might mean that the PFD won't do its job, however, so fasten and tighten the belly strap and use thigh straps if they are fitted.

PFDs also serve a secondary purpose on a fishing kayak, and that is for transporting some of your safety kit. There are many items that have to be on your person and can't be stashed on the kayak. There are (rather dubious) stories of instructors seeing pupils with so much stuff attached to their PFDs that the PFD sinks under its own weight. However, it is worth going for just a little extra buoyancy when buying the jacket to allow for the weight of some extra gear. PFDs are rated in terms of Newtons of buoyancy; more is generally better.

The Kaikoura is a popular PFD and the radio pocket is a great feature. Photo: palmequipmenteurope.com

Also think about what you are going to be wearing when you go out on the kayak. In summer you might just be wearing a wetsuit but in the winter it might be a dry suit and three or four layers of clothing. Your PFD therefore has to be adjustable to cope with both sets of clothing.

One thing I look for in a PFD is the ability to put a water bladder into the back pocket. You can end up dehydrated very easily at sea, and having a source of water available at all times is a very useful feature.

Some PFDs can be fitted with a hydration pack, a useful way of avoiding dehydration while paddling.

Something else to look for is a radio pocket. Some PFDs come with a dedicated radio pocket for a handheld VHF with a hole for the aerial to poke out, and I've found these very useful. Most PFDs nowadays come complete with a whistle already attached, but if your model doesn't then a cheap plastic whistle can be bought for just a few pounds. It is a great method of attracting attention to yourself and can just be left in the pocket of the PFD where, hopefully, you will never need it.

If your PFD doesn't come with a whistle then get yourself one.

Off the leash

Along with a PFD, the other item that the instructor on my course insisted upon is a paddle leash. Basically, this is just a length of cord which is secured to the paddle at one end and is clipped or tied onto the kayak at the other. A paddle leash is important because it ensures that, if you fall off and keep hold of your paddle, then you (and the paddle) will stay attached to your kayak. There is nothing worse than falling in and keeping hold of the kayak only to discover that your paddle has drifted away out of reach.

I prefer the type of leash that either attaches to the kayak with a loop or is fitted with a carabiner-type clip. Some cheap leashes come with a plastic clip, but these are best avoided since I've had some come undone on occasion. Velcro collars around the paddle shaft work well, although leashes with just a loop of bungee cord and a moveable toggle are also acceptable.

A paddle leash is an essential part of your safety equipment.

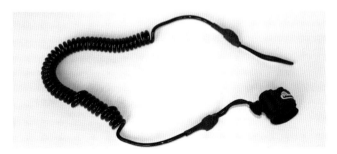

Some people also like to leash themselves to their kayak, but I wouldn't recommend this if you are going anywhere near surf.

Being attached by a line to a tumbling kayak is not amusing. On the other hand, if you are anchoring in a strong current or fishing alone at night, then some method of attaching yourself to your kayak can be useful. Several manufacturers make coiled-up leashes that can be worn on your belt and are tucked away until you need them. This type of leash is quite comfortable to wear. I've seen someone walk away from their kayak forgetting all about their leash, only to come to an abrupt halt a few metres away.

Knives

The other item that I always take fishing with me is a decent knife. I carry it attached to my PFD so that if I end up in the water and tangled in lines I can quickly cut myself free. A knife can also come in handy for getting rid of your anchor in a hurry should the need arise. It's best to carry a proper rescue knife with a rounded tip to the blade so you can't stab yourself by accident. Buy either the folding type and attach it to your PFD with a lanyard, or the type in a quick release scabbard which you can mount on your PFD.

A very sharp (but blunt ended) rescue knife, attached to your PFD where you can easily reach it, is a must.

Some anglers also carry a knife down the side of their boot, diver style, working on the theory that this would be the best place for a knife if your feet became tangled in lines after falling in. Knives other than safety knives on kayaks are generally not a great idea. Many anglers don't carry a filleting knife for dealing with fish but instead carry bait scissors; that way you can be sure you won't cut yourself before being faced with a long paddle home.

RNLI advice

Once you've got yourself a PFD and a paddle leash it's time to think about what else you might need. I always defer to the RNLI on matters of safety; after all, it's these guys who will have to come and get you if it all goes wrong. The RNLI publishes a leaflet specifically for kayak safety and this can be downloaded from their website (rnli.org.uk).

The RNLI kit advice is split into two sections: one for sheltered inshore paddling and one covering the stuff you'll need when you start to venture further afield.

For inshore trips, the RNLI recommends 'a suitable means of calling for help' and mentions either a portable VHF or flares. Although they're excellent for back-up, a mobile phone (even the waterproof variety) isn't up to the job.

Once you start to venture further afield then the list gets longer. The RNLI recommends a two-piece spare paddle, a waterproof torch with working batteries, a waterproof GPS, a waterproof compass and a waterproof watch, a tow rope, a basic first aid kit, sunscreen/sunglasses/sunhat, spare clothes and an exposure/survival bag.

Handheld VHF

A marine VHF will tell everyone in the vicinity that there is a problem and will enable you to talk directly to the rescue services. It also has the advantage that you can listen in to other boat users, often other fishermen, and can even talk to your mates in other kayaks. You will find that almost all kayak anglers carry a handheld VHF.

A mobile phone makes a good back-up communication device, but will need to be kept inside a waterproof pouch.

It's worth noting that you should carry your radio on your PFD and not on your kayak. It's no good mounting the radio on the kayak, only to watch kayak and radio drift away after an accident. See p86 for more information on portable VHF radios.

Flares

You'll also find that most serious kayak anglers also carry flares as well as a handheld VHF radio. The most popular flares by far are an inshore pack, usually carried on the kayak itself. These packs normally comprise a couple of handheld red flares, as well as a couple of handheld smoke flares. They nearly always come in a waterproof tube which is easily attached to the tackle box or crate that most people carry in their tank well.

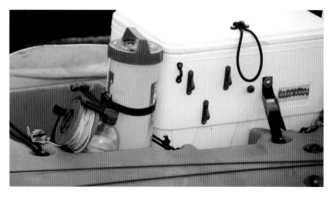

An inshore flare pack can be attached to your fishing crate.

While the inshore pack is excellent, some anglers also carry personal flares attached to their PFD or in a pocket. In the case of being separated from the kayak, they then still have flares available to call for help. The combined day and night personal flare, which sells for around £40, is again a very popular choice. Flares have a limited shelf life and the dates are usually clearly marked on the packaging. It's worth checking your flares from time to time to make sure that they are still useable.

Spare paddle

How would you cope if your paddle was damaged or lost? Spare paddles can be bought for around £40 and I always carry one with me. The problem with your spare paddle, however, is that it has to be somewhere you can get hold of it in a hurry. On some kayaks, there will be hatches that are safe to open at sea which also have good seals. On these kayaks you can carry the spare paddle in the hull of the boat. On others, however, it isn't possible to access the main hatches at sea and it might be better to strap your spare paddle to your tank well.

When I started I just chucked my spare into the hull. I found that it tended to become wedged at one end or the other, requiring me to stand the kayak on its nose and give it a good thump to loosen the paddle. Needless to say, this is not something you'd want to attempt at sea. Nowadays, I've fitted a collar to the spare paddle and tied it to a convenient point just inside my centre hatch.

Lights

It may seem a little like overkill for the RNLI to insist on you having some form of light with you, as many people only fish during the day. However, if anything goes wrong towards the end of the trip it can be very easy to find yourself afloat after dark. The RNLI recommends a waterproof torch with fully charged batteries.

You'll find that many kayak anglers also carry a strobe light attached to their PFD. These can be purchased for anything from £10 upwards depending on the model. Some strobes will be marketed as 'SOLAS approved'. This is the International Convention for the Safety of Life at Sea, and is one of the awarding bodies for safety at sea. SOLAS-rated products tend to be expensive, but they have passed stringent criteria.

Compass

With a GPS in the recommended kit list, you might question the need to carry an old-fashioned compass as well. The reason is simply that GPS systems can – and do – go wrong. If you carry a compass then you've always got a back-up. The most common use for a compass on a kayak is for steering a particular course, for example after the fog has come down and you are trying to find your way home.

There are a wide variety of compasses available, many now marketed for kayaks. These can be either permanently fixed in place on the deck or held in place over a hatch with bungee straps. Please note that compasses are readily affected by metal items such as batteries and fish finders; it's important to make sure that your compass is working correctly once it has been installed.

As well as a so-called steering compass you'll find many anglers also carry a bearing compass with them, often in a pocket of their PFD. A bearing compass is a device that enables the user to take a bearing of an object. This object could be something fixed ashore for navigational purposes or, if the worst comes to the worst, someone in distress so that you can report their position to the emergency services.

The RNLI also recommends that you plan your trip and carry the appropriate trip plan with you, as well as appropriate charts. See p70 for details of trip planning and using charts.

EPIRB

The final piece of safety kit you may wish to consider for your kayak is an EPIRB, an Emergency Position Indicating Radio Beacon. These units have become much more affordable recently and, although probably overkill for the inshore fisherman, one of these tucked away in your PFD would be a good form of insurance if you are thinking about regularly paddling long distances.

As with many things on a kayak, they are likely to get wet. Steer clear of those which are automatically activated on contact with water and go for one with manual activation instead. If you do get an EPIRB for your kayak, then it should be registered with the relevant search and rescue authorities.

Common sense

This huge list of equipment might seem like overkill, as I'm sure that there are some of you out there who just want to paddle out from the beach in your swimming trunks and catch a few mackerel. The problem with this approach is that you are going out to sea. The sea is unpredictable and can change very rapidly, even with a good weather forecast.

It makes sense to think long and hard about safety before you go out to sea. You should always seek the appropriate training as well as advice about kit. You can then relax and enjoy yourself knowing that, if the unexpected does occur, you have planned to cope with the worst.

FITTING OUT YOUR KAYAK

Photo: Mark Crame

There are two schools of thought when it comes to fitting out a kayak. The more traditional kayakers, who are coming to fishing from kayaking, will probably want to keep everything as simple as possible. Anglers coming to kayak fishing, however, are probably going to go after some toys.

Since you are using your kayak to catch fish, you are going to have to fit some basic stuff to the kayak to help you feel safe and comfortable when you are out fishing.

Nowadays there are a lot of angler-friendly kayak designs. You can obtain a fully fitted fishing kayak, ideal for those not handy with a drill and silicon sealant. It's worth looking at the various items being offered in the package, however, and working out what they would cost if you were to fit them yourself. It is possible to make substantial savings by buying the stuff separately. Some dealers will even fit stuff for you so can have the best of both worlds.

Rod rests

The most obvious accessory is somewhere to put your rod. At the kayak shows you'll often see kayaks fitted out with goodness knows how many rods sticking out at every conceivable angle. It's worth thinking about just how many rods you intend taking afloat at any one time. Indeed, there is a part of me that doesn't really approve of rod rests. Some of my best fishing has been with just a single lure rod or a live eel on the drift. In both instances, the last thing you want to do is to put the rod down. However, there comes a time when you are going to want to take more than one rod afloat and even fish with more than one. This is when you are going to have to think about drilling a few holes into your beloved kayak and fitting a rod holder.

(Below) a RAM mount. (Right) Twin RAM mounts are a popular choice, and can be swung forward when fishing. This kayak also has a home made double rod rest fitted to the front of the cockpit.

When you buy your kayak, the chances are you will offered a pair of flush mounted holders behind the seat and perhaps the ubiquitous Scotty mount fixed at the front of the cockpit. This set-up, although very common, has a couple of drawbacks. Firstly, although flush mounts do hold rods securely, they also fill up with water. Secondly, and more importantly, they leave your reel very close to the water which isn't a great idea in the long term.

RAM rod holder

If outfitting from scratch, I now prefer to use one of the Round-A-Mount (RAM) excellent tubular rod holders. Not only do they hold the reel a long way above the water, but the ball and socket joint enables them to be swung right forward for fishing at anchor, as well as out to the sides for trolling and pointing towards the rear for transit. The RAM 119 fits onto a plate which has a 1.5 inch rubber ball. They can be easily removed leaving just the ball attached to the kayak, although a friend of mine does have a couple of ball-shaped dents in the roof of his car from loading his kayak a little too enthusiastically.

They come in two varieties: a plastic version and an aluminium version. The metal version is more expensive, but is slightly easier to lock up really tight. The only downside of RAM mounts for fishing tackle is that they aren't as widely available as other systems (e.g. Scotty or Berkley).

Position

I find the best place for the holder is just behind the seat, so that when swung forward the reels come nicely to hand at the side of the kayak.

The Scotty Baitcaster is a popular rod rest, but can be a little small for heavier rod butts.
Photo: scotty.com

If you are offered a kayak with a Scotty rod holder fitted at the front of the kayak, make sure you know which type it is. Some Scotties are designed for the American market where people use very light rods, so you may find that British sea fishing rods won't fit. Another thing to consider is whether you are able to reach this forward-fitted Scotty. If you get the chance, sit in the cockpit and make sure you can get a rod out of the holder.

I admit I did neither of these things when I bought my kayak and ended up not only with a rod holder which was too small for my rods, but one which was also out of my reach even if I could have got a rod into it. I got around this by using the base for something else. The Scotty system has all sorts of fittings, including one for a fish finder mounting which I used for a while before eventually converting the Scotty base to another RAM mount ball.

For those of you with longer arms who can reach a forward-mounted Scotty, they do a very good triple mount bar which turns a single mounting point into a triple mounting point.

Scotty's triple rod holder is very popular; this one is fitted with three power lock rod holders but it's often seen with a fish finder on the central mount.
Photo: scotty.com

Nuts and bolts

Once you've decided where you want to put the rod rests, and what type of rest you are going to fit, then it's time to look at how you attach them to the kayak. A lot will depend on where you decide to put the fittings and how easy it is to reach inside the hull. If there is a convenient hatch through which you can reach the inside of the hull, then the best way to attach a fitting is to use a stainless steel bolt through the fitting and through the hull. Attach a stainless steel washer and a locking nut inside the hull.

Not only is it important to use stainless steel fittings on a kayak, it's also really important to get the right kind of stainless steel. Most of the stuff you will find in the DIY stores is what is known as A2 stainless steel and this simply isn't corrosion-resistant enough for use in the harsh conditions to which it will be subjected on a kayak. You'll need to search a bit to track down A4 stainless steel fittings and have to pay around twice as much, but they are really worth it. The best place to look is usually chandlery stores.

Some kayaks can seem a little thin when you are bolting stuff to them, particularly if you want to bolt a fitting away from a designated fitting point. You can reinforce these areas with a backing board if you are attaching the fitting to a flat part of the hull. Buy a nylon chopping board for a couple of pounds and simply cut out a piece larger than the footprint of the attachment. Drill holes for each of the bolts, and then fit the piece of chopping board inside the hull. Use the bolts to clamp the hull between the fitting and the backing board. This can be really useful if fitting rod rests where you expect there to be some force exerted on the fitting.

Riveting stuff

Things become a little more complicated if you can't get access to the inside of your kayak where you want to attach a fitting. The first thing to check is that there isn't already a threaded moulding in that area. Some kayaks have loads of spare attachment points, so you might get lucky and not need to drill any more holes.

Stainless steel rivets can be used to attach all sorts of things to your kayak.

Assuming that there isn't an attachment point that you can borrow, you are left with two main ways of attaching a fitting: using a rivet or using well nuts. If the fitting you are going to attach is relatively slim, then rivets can work really well. Those to look for are the black anodized tri-fold pop rivets with a silicone seal and neoprene gasket. Don't be tempted to use normal metal working rivets, as these may well leak or damage the hull of the kayak. They're quite expensive but you'll not need many and they can usually be bought in small packs from your friendly local kayak emporium.

Good rivets will be aircraft grade, and provide a large bearing surface with a silicone seal and neoprene gasket that resists pull outs, leakage or cracking when set in plastics and other brittle or soft materials. If you don't think that is enough then some people also put a small drop of marine silicon sealant into the hole before inserting the rivet. I must admit I usually go for this belt-and-braces approach myself when fitting deck hardware.

To fix the cleat, mark the two
holes and then drill holes
to accept the well nuts.
The cleat is then bolted down
onto the well nuts, which
expand to make a seal. A
little sealant is added to
make sure it is waterproof.

If you don't fancy using rivets or if the fitting you are trying to attach is particularly deep (e.g. a cleat), then another method is to use a device known as a well nut. This consists of a stainless steel or a brass nut at the bottom of rubber tube with a flange at the top. You drill a hole the same diameter as the rubber tube, and insert the well nut so that it is retained by its flange. If you then tighten a stainless steel bolt through the fitting, the nut will be pulled up and form a theoretically water tight seal inside the hull. I've found well nuts to be very effective and they can take a decent load, but they do require you to drill some large holes in your kayak. Again, a dab of sealant makes sure the joint is doubly watertight.

Storage crates

Once you've finished screwing, bolting and riveting all those carefully chosen accessories to your kayak it's time to think about how you are going to transport your fishing gear. Almost all fishing kayaks come with some form of tank well behind the seat, and most people end up buying some form of free-draining plastic crate to fit into the tank well. A free-draining crate is a better idea than a box because (a) it won't fill with water in the event of large waves and (b) it won't be affected by the wind as much as a solid box.

You can pick up this type of crate for a few pounds at any of the major DIY sheds, and a lot of them also fold for storage when you've taken them off the kayak. There's no need to attach them with anything other than the bungee cords that come with most kayaks. Because the water will just run through them, a crate on the back of a kayak also makes sense should you ever have to right the kayak after a capsize.

Once you've got a crate it's very easy to use cable ties to attach further items of tackle or accessories to the sides of the crate. Tubular rod holders can be made out of convenient lengths of plastic piping. Heat the tubing with a hair dryer or heat gun and then create a flared mouth by pushing the hot plastic tube down over a beer bottle for a really professional finish. Alternatively, you can buy a set of three for around a tenner from most chandlers.

I also used to attach a filleting knife to my crate and had a plastic cutting board pushed into the back. I've since changed my mind about this and now carry a pair of bait scissors which are less likely to inflict an injury. After all, it would be a very painful paddle home with a cut on your hand.

On my own crate I've added a simple stainless steel T-bar type disgorger, which stays on the crate and means that I don't forget to take one with me when I go to sea. Discovering you've forgotten the T-bar when unhooking an unhappy conger can end in tears!

What you put in the crate is really up to you. I've ended up with a small(ish) tackle box for a few leads and some traces, and sometimes another plastic box for my lunch. When I first started kayaking I tended to take far too much stuff out with me, and was constantly rummaging around behind me looking for things. After you've been out a few times you learn that you can fish with the simplest of rigs and the minimum of tackle. Often, I can put enough gear into the pockets of my PFD that I don't need to reach behind me at all. In my case, less is definitely more when it comes to enjoying my fishing.

On a final note it's always worth thinking about what would happen if you did fall in. Would you be able to right the kayak with all your gear on it? Anything not attached to the kayak is going on a one-way trip to the bottom, so if it's not tied on then you've got to be prepared to lose it. Making sure you fit leashes to all your rods is a bit like backing up your computer – you know you should but you never get around to it until you lose the lot. I'm sure the seabed is littered with kayaker's lost fishing rods, so leash it or lose it.

Rudders

The final piece of outfitting I'm going to cover is a rudder. Although aftermarket rudders are available, it's probably best to buy a rudder from the same maker as your kayak to ensure a proper fit. A lot of kayaks are sold as rudder ready, and some even have all the tubing installed inside the hull so fitting a rudder is a simple job. I personally haven't bothered fitting a rudder as I find that, with the type of fishing I do, I don't need one. Purists will argue that its better to learn to paddle without one rather than relying on a rudder to correct poor technique, but it's down to personal choice.

Adding a rudder can make handling easier; pictured is the outsize rudder fitted to the Ocean Kayak Torque.

Hanging out

Once you've got your kayak fitted out, there is just one more thing to cover and that's storage of your kayak. For the greatest longevity, you should store your kayak out of direct sunlight (although most manufacturers use pretty good UV inhibitors these days so this isn't as much of an issue as it used to be). Provided you are going to store your kayak indoors there are a couple of options: either get some form of rack (usually in the form of two stout brackets that bolt to the wall) or go for some kind of hoist system.

I went for a hoist system whereby my kayak is stored safely out of the way in the roof space of my garage but can easily be lowered onto the waiting C-Tug. I use four pulleys which effectively halves the weight of the kayak, allowing me to pull it up and down on my own. I used a cheap nylon line to make the rigging, and padded the slings with a few off-cuts from an old hose pipe to spread the load a little.

My kayak stored in the roof of the garage.

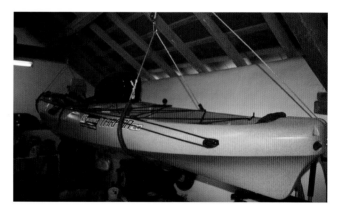

Keeping kayaks flat is the best way to store them. Make sure that the slings are relatively close together so that the boat is supported in the middle and not by the ends. Don't be tempted to hang the kayak by the grab hands as this can distort the hull.

My kayak

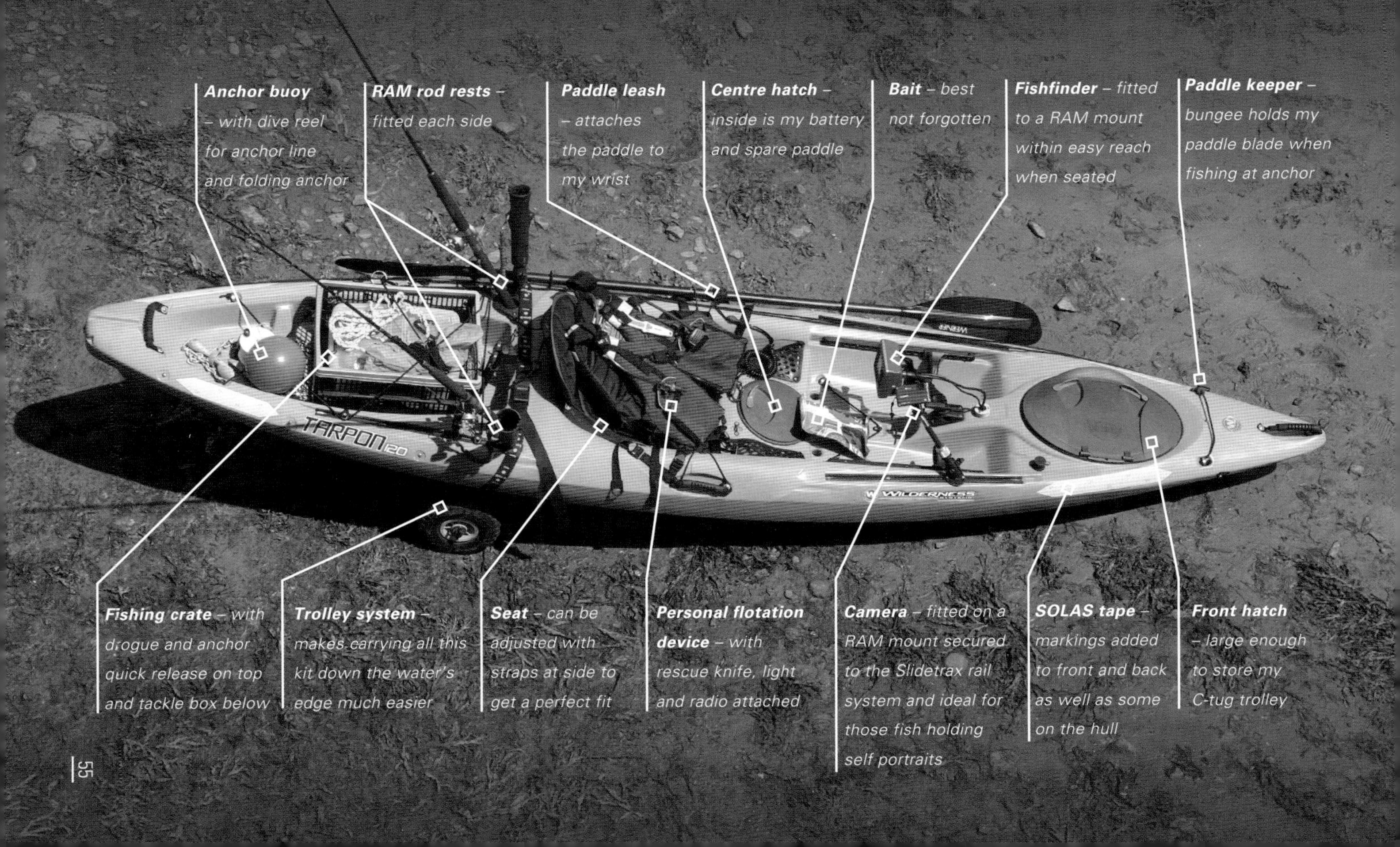

Paddle keeper – bungee holds my paddle blade when fishing at anchor

Front hatch – large enough to store my C-tug trolley

Fishfinder – fitted to a RAM mount within easy reach when seated

SOLAS tape – markings added to front and back as well as some on the hull

Bait – best not forgotten

Camera – fitted on a RAM mount secured to the Slidetrax rail system and ideal for those fish holding self portraits

Centre hatch – inside is my battery and spare paddle

Paddle leash – attaches the paddle to my wrist

Personal flotation device – with rescue knife, light and radio attached

RAM rod rests – fitted each side

Seat – can be adjusted with straps at side to get a perfect fit

Anchor buoy – with dive reel for anchor line and folding anchor

Trolley system – makes carrying all this kit down the water's edge much easier

Fishing crate – with drogue and anchor quick release on top and tackle box below

55

KAYAKING WITH CONFIDENCE

With your new kayak and all the necessary safety kit, you're now keen to go fishing. Where should you start? Without doubt you should start by getting some training under your belt. The best way to do this is to find a local kayaking coach who runs SOT training sessions. These needn't be expensive, and a day's coaching can often be had for £100 or so.

For an even cheaper option, you might find that your local dealer runs free come-and-try days for people who are thinking of buying a kayak. While this kind of session isn't a substitute for proper coaching, it does let you meet others new to the sport and try out a number of kayaks in a very controlled environment.

Your instructor will show you how to get back onto a SOT.

The most important thing you'll learn on one of these courses is how to get back on the kayak should you fall in. There is absolutely nothing to be afraid of when it comes to falling in. Getting back onto a sit-on-top kayak is extremely easy, but it's vital that you get a bit of practice under your belt before having to do it for real.

Once you've got some training under your belt the next thing to think about is finding someone else to fish with. When you are first starting out it's a great idea to fish with someone else from a safety point of view. Even as your skills progress you may still want to fish with other people (if only to have someone else there to take the catch photographs).

Many of the kayak fishing websites organise events where you can meet other kayak anglers and see how they've rigged their kayaks.

Training ideas

Although I can provide a few tips here, I strongly suggest that you take a few lessons. Look on the internet for a local kayaking coach and book a one-to-one session. Alternatively, join a local club or book yourself a place on one of the increasing number of sit-on-top training courses that are springing up around the country. Whatever you decide to do, make sure you get the basics sorted before you decide to venture out for the first time. A fully loaded fishing kayak anchored in a strong tide is not the place to be attempting your first self-rescue.

There are also some very good books out there, and I highly recommend *Sit-on-Top Kayak* by Jersey's Derek Hairon. I read this book from cover to cover several times when I was starting out. It has some very good step-by-step photo sequences that will help you get your head around how to control a kayak. (If you're anything like me, it will also leave you lusting after a kayaking course on Jersey.)

The British Canoe Union (BCU) tends to get a lot of bad press for not being oriented to the needs of kayak anglers, but it is all we've got. Joining a BCU club therefore has to be a good idea and can be great way to meet fellow paddlers. The BCU also runs a series of award schemes. Again, these tend not to be aimed at kayak anglers, but the one and two star awards cover pretty basic kayaking and are well worth signing up for. If you become hooked, you may even end up trying to collect all the awards or even going onto instructor-level qualifications.

Forward paddling

You might think that paddling in a straight line should be a relatively easy task. It seems fairly simple on the face of it – the blades are the same size so why wouldn't you just head off in a straight line? Well, not quite. When starting off, most people find it quite difficult to paddle a sit-on-top in a straight line. This is easy enough to correct by just adding a few extra strokes on one side. In the longer term, however, you want to learn to steer the boat without using extra correction strokes. These can break your rhythm, which can make paddling longer distances more tiring.

Many kayaks have the provision to fit a rudder, and this is an easy way to ensure you go in a straight line. However, I think that learning to paddle properly using a good coach to teach you correct technique is a better idea than fitting a rudder to correct poor technique.

When the wind blows from the side it will try to turn the boat. Holding the paddle off centre can help counteract this. Photo: from Sit-on-Top Kayak by Derek Hairon.

I'm certainly not a kayaking coach, but there are a couple of ways to make the boat change direction without a rudder or using extra strokes. One is to hold the paddle off-centre, so that one blade has a longer distance to travel than the other and thus more leverage. It's worth playing around with this – if you consistently veer to one side, then slightly offsetting the paddle can correct it.

The other method involves leaning on one of your foot pegs. If you paddle with more pressure on one foot than the other while keeping your body upright, you'll find that the kayak will naturally start to turn. Again, seek out the services of a good coach and get out on the water and practise. You will find that this technique is often more than enough to correct any wandering tendencies.

Paddling can be quite an exhausting activity, so it pays to build up your paddle fitness gradually. Start by going out for just a short trip, and gradually build up the length of time you're afloat and paddling. You'll be amazed at how quickly you can build up your stamina.

Self-rescue

I suggest that at least once a year you find the time to go out and practise recovery drills. The more you practise, the more it will become second nature and the less likely it will be that you come to harm if it happens for real. It's also well worth going out and doing a few recovery drills every time you change a major piece of gear (e.g. PFD or a dry suit), to prove that you can still get back on top of the kayak with the new equipment.

When it comes to getting back onto an overturned kayak, I was taught a simple pneumonic for remembering the various steps involved at an Anglers Afloat training session: GUT, which stands for Grab, Upturn and Think.

Grab is the first thing you do if you end up in the water, and simply means grab hold of your paddle or kayak so that you don't become separated. Your paddle should always be securely leashed to your kayak, so grabbing your paddle will also keep you in contact with your kayak.

The next stage is to quickly **upturn** your kayak. Kayaks aren't designed to spend long periods of time upside down in the water and, although some hatches are markedly better than others, it makes sense to get your kayak floating the right way up as quickly as possible. When it comes to righting your kayak, you may find it better to reach under the kayak, grab the far edge and then pull it towards you, which can be better than trying to flip the kayak over by lifting the edge closest to you. If you do go for the lifting approach, the kayak can fail to turn completely over and might come back down on your head! Always turn the yak over with the wind behind you, so it helps rather than hinders the process.

Pause to catch your breath and collect your thoughts. Make sure there is nothing cluttering up the seat or part of the kayak that you want to climb back onto and that any fishing tackle is secure and out of the way. **Think** about how best to climb back on.

Going out for a splash around, practicing self rescues and testing out new kit isn't a chore, it's great fun. Photo: Nick Webb.

Getting back on should then be a simple matter of grabbing the side of the kayak and then kicking with your legs to climb on board, rather like getting out onto the edge of a swimming pool. You may find it easier to get your legs close to the surface of the water before you start kicking, rather than having them below you, but this is a matter of personal choice. Once the tops of your legs are just above the side of the kayak, it is a fairly simple matter to just roll over. This will leave you sitting in the kayak with your legs dangling over the edge, and is a very stable position. From this position, it should be easy to move your legs around and swing them back into the kayak. **Think** about how you are going to get back on easily and sort everything out before you haul yourself out of the water.

Some trainers try to teach you to do the whole thing in one graceful manoeuvre, but I find it a lot easier to take it step by step and pause when I'm halfway into the kayak with my legs over the side.

Practice really does make perfect. I've fished with some people who have never fallen in and it actually makes them rather stilted in their handling of the kayak. Once you've been in a good few times you realise there is nothing to be worried about and you become much more fluid in your movements. Everyone falls in at some point, so it makes huge sense to find out how to do it in a controlled environment and at your own pace. That way, when it does happen for real, it won't come as a complete shock.

If there are two of you, then you can help the other person get back onto the kayak. This is another reason why it is a good idea to fish with at least one other angler.

Leave the rod at home

Before you go fishing for the first time, try to carry out a recon-naissance trip without any of your gear on board. This will enable you to become familiar with your kayak without any fishing dis-tractions. Most importantly, it can allow you to practise a few recoveries before fully loading the kayak with all your gear.

Even after you've been out fishing a few times, it's still a really good idea to go out every once in a while without any fishing gear and just have a play in the kayak. If you have surf beaches near you, a surfing session with an unloaded boat can be great fun. By pushing yourself and your kayak, you will find the limits of both and gain valuable knowledge that you can use the next time you are fishing.

Paddle plan

Some form of paddle plan is a very good idea to help you prepare for the trip. You should look at who is going, where you are going to launch from, agree a radio channel that you can use to communicate, make a note of the tides and currents expected for the area and time you are going to fish and check the weather for the period you are intending to fish.

Adding some kind of formality to this process can ensure that you don't forget to check something vital. Many kayakers write it all down before they go, which also gives you a great record of your outings for the year.

Coastguard communication

Before you get down to fishing, it might be a good idea to register your kayak with the coastguard under their CG66 scheme. This scheme is a voluntary database of all the craft around the UK and contains details about your kayak (including a photo of it), the safety equipment you are carrying, your radio call sign and, most importantly, your contact details.

The details can be found online at mcga.gov.uk. You can fill out the form online, where you can also upload a photo of your kayak. You can also download and print out the entry form and then simply pop it in the post addressed to your nearest coastguard centre (a list of which can be found on the MCA website).

When you do go out for a trip it is vital that you tell someone where you are going and when you intend to return. Tell a friend or relative so that they can raise the alarm if you don't return on time, and also tell your local coastguard station. Don't be worried that you will be bothering the coastguard by telling them you are going out for a paddle – you'll usually find them very friendly. By telling them who is going, how many kayaks there are, where you are going to be fishing and what time you are due to come back, you can give them a huge head start if anything does go wrong. However, don't forget to phone up when you get out of the water and tell them that you've finished!

You can inform the coastguard of your plans over your radio, but I always find it easier and more convenient to use the phone (signal permitting). You don't legally have to do this, but I always try to ensure that the coastguard knows where I am.

Find a fishing buddy

The internet is a great place to meet fellow newbies to the sport. Most sites will have a section dedicated to newcomers, or at least a section where people can post the dates of any planned trips. The kayaking world is, in my experience, a very friendly one. I was amazed at the reaction from other kayak fishermen when I sent tentative emails asking if I could come along on trips. Far from telling me to bugger off, I got loads of advice and a warm welcome. Everyone was very keen to show me how they did things and how they used their kit.

The hobby is still very new and everyone is learning. I think that this plays a large part in making it such a fun activity, and also explains why others are so keen to share (unlike shore angling which seems to have become more secretive over the last decade).

Fishing with a friend is a good habit to get into, particularly when you are starting off.

SEAMANSHIP FOR KAYAK ANGLERS

Photo: Nick Webb.

One question that is bound to crop up is: just what are safe conditions? This is an often-asked question and one which is impossible to answer. It all depends on a vast quantity of different considerations: the paddler, the kayak, the wind direction, the possibilities of shelter and the state of the tide.

In short, I think the best advice is to start with calm conditions with no waves and no wind. Gradually build up your experience by trying conditions which are a little more challenging. Push yourself that little bit further, preferably in the company of someone who knows what they are doing. The sea is a far from stable environment, and its ever-changing nature means that is it vital you understand the processes going on around you.

When you start kayaking, pick calm days with small tides and gradually build up to more challenging conditions.

Standing on a beach, often after a long drive, deciding whether or not to go out is sometimes difficult. If in doubt, don't go out. You'll be able to come back another day, so better safe than sorry.

Weather

Obtaining a decent, detailed weather forecast for the area you are planning to fish is a vital part of trip planning. Just because it's flat calm and still when you set out doesn't mean it's going to stay that way.

A factor which you must take very seriously is wind speed and direction. The amount by which the wind can affect a kayaker depends on the size of the paddler, the cross-section of the kayak and how loaded the kayak is. If the wind is going in the same direction as the tide, then the chances are that the sea will be flatter than if the wind and tide are going in different directions. 'Wind against tide' often throws up the worst seas which can be highly changeable.

The BBC inshore weather forecasts are a good starting point, but you really need a more detailed local forecast. There are a number of very good weather websites out there. I've tended to gravitate towards those sites that are aimed at either surfers or windsurfers. One of my favourites is Windguru, which is free for the basic information. It provides a decent forecast for the week ahead with wave height and period along with the more usual wind speed and direction. Magicseaweed is another site well worth adding to your favourites bar.

Last, but by no means least, is the good old-fashioned shipping forecast. While afloat, tune into the local coastguard on channel 16 and listen out for the channel announcement. Times of local forecasts vary, and it's worth checking the coastguard website to find the broadcast times for your area.

Tides

The main factor affecting the tides is the position of the moon relative to the earth and sun. Imagine that the earth is uniformly covered with water. The gravitational pull of the moon causes a 'bulge' in this layer where it is closest to the moon and an equal and opposite bulge on the other side of the planet. Since the earth is rotating on its axis once a day, every area passes through both of these two bulges each day. (The tidal cycle is not exactly 24 hours because the moon is also orbiting the earth over a period of a month.)

When the earth, sun and moon are lined up (i.e. full moon or new moon), the sun and the moon combine to create bigger 'bulges' which correspond to spring tides. At first or third quarter, the sun counteracts some of the effect of the moon and we experience neap tides.

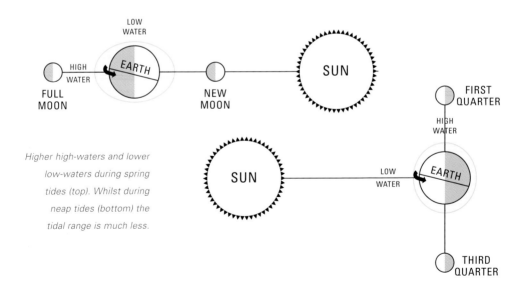

Higher high-waters and lower low-waters during spring tides (top). Whilst during neap tides (bottom) the tidal range is much less.

Tidal range

The change in water levels over the tidal cycle (tidal range) can vary enormously around the country from tens of metres in the Bristol Channel to just a few metres in some favoured estuaries. This change in height isn't constant, however, but is slower around the time of low or high water and faster halfway between.

An approximate method of estimating by how much the tidal range will change over any hour is by using the '**rule of twelfths**'. This states that in the first hour after low (high) water, the water height will rise (fall) by one-twelfth of the total range. In the second hour after low (high) water, the water height will rise (fall) by two-twelfths. The height will change by three-twelfths during both the third and fourth hours and, during the fifth and sixth hours, the height will change by two-twelfths and one-twelfth, respectively.

Rule of twelfths: Estimating the change in the height of water by the hour.

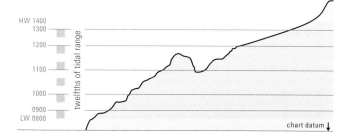

Although being able to predict the tidal height at any time is useful for e.g. divers wanting to explore a wreck or for knowing how far up the beach you need to leave your kayak, information about the strength and direction of the tidal stream is more useful when paddling on the sea.

Tidal stream

If you know the maximum rate (in knots) at spring tides, you can use the '**rule of thirds**' to estimate the average speed of the tidal stream at any time. During the first and sixth hours after slack water, the average speed of the tidal current will be one-third that of the maximum spring rate. It will be two-thirds the maximum rate during the second and fifth hours, and will be equal to the maximum rate during both the third and fourth hours.

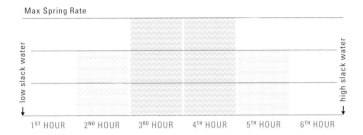

Max Spring Rate

low slack water

high slack water

1ST HOUR   2ND HOUR   3RD HOUR   4TH HOUR   5TH HOUR   6TH HOUR

The maximum tidal current observed during neap tides is half that of springs. For example, for a given maximum spring rate of 6 knots, you could calculate that at 2 hours after low water during neaps tides, the current will be 2 knots (half of 6 knots multiplied by 2/3).

Sources of tidal information

Although most places will have a fairly simple tidal pattern with roughly six hours between successive low and high tides, tidal flow can also be a very complicated affair. Knowing the exact tide times for where you are going to fish is important. Tide times for a particular port can be found on the BBC website, or there is a very good free website easytide.ukho.gov.uk. Most seaside tackle shops will also sell tide tables for the coming year.

If you want to know what the tidal currents in a particular area will be doing in terms of direction and strength, you will have to invest in an Admiralty Tidal Stream Atlas. These break the UK down into manageable chunks and provide the strength and direction of the current at hourly intervals.

The tidal stream atlas which covers my local area.

Planning your fishing trip in this way can really save you a lot of time and hard work. If you plan properly, you can use the tide instead of fighting against it. Such planning is particularly useful as you start to travel longer distances in search of good fishing.

Although a tidal atlas gives good data, the maps are usually fairly large-scale and most of the data refers to points quite a long way offshore. You'll often want more detailed information about conditions closer inshore.

The best source of tidal information can often be by word-of-mouth from local fishermen or anglers who know the area extremely well. Having fished the area countless times, they should be able to provide first-hand information.

Another good source of advice is the Admiralty Pilot for the area in question, which provides detailed information particularly around the mouths of rivers and ports.

Finally, there is often very good information to be found in kayaking guide books. Books which are aimed at assisting you to plan relatively long passages around the coastline give very detailed tidal advice which can come in handy for planning fishing trips.

There is an obvious safety aspect to knowing what current to expect and from which direction. Even a fit paddler with a decent touring sit-on-top will struggle to keep up a prolonged speed of much over 3 knots. It's therefore vital to ensure that you don't end up paddling into a current stronger than this or else you'll end up going backwards! You also need to factor in the speed of the current when you are estimating how long it will take to get somewhere. Either add or subtract the current (if it is with you or against you) to your estimated paddling speed to give you a rough idea of actual speed.

Sea kayak guidebooks often have good inshore tidal stream information which can be hard to find elsewhere.

Reading charts

I won't go into huge detail about charts here (there are several good books for that, including *Sea Kayak Navigation* by Franco Ferrero) but you should familiarise yourself with the basics and learn how to turn the series of numbers given to you by your GPS into a position on the chart.

The British Admiralty is the aquatic equivalent of the Ordnance Survey, and publishes many different types of UK charts. For kayakers I find that the tough chart series is ideal; it is a collection of relatively small waterproof charts which come in portfolios covering sections of the coastline.

Charts can also be amazingly useful for prospecting new fishing marks, and often show features such as wrecks, sand banks and drop offs, all of which are well worth investigating.

Charts will tell you something about the likely sea conditions where you are going to fish. Tidal diamonds are accompanied by a table which lists the direction and strength of the tidal stream over a period of approximately 12 hours (from one low water to the next).

Tidal arrows, usually in pairs, indicate the direction of the ebb and flood (the feathered arrow describing the flood direction). The arrows are usually accompanied by an indication of the speed of the flow. If there is just one figure, it refers to the maximum speed you can expect during spring tides in tenths of a knot i.e. '21' would imply a tidal stream of strength 2.1 knots. If there are two figures, then the smaller figure refers to the flow during neaps.

Overfalls – something to be avoided when starting out – are indicated on a chart by pairs of squiggly lines. Usually indicated around headlands or where a channel narrows, they are caused by the squeezing of a tidal stream either around an obstruction or through a channel. Although more experienced kayakers may describe them as 'fun', overfalls can be unpredictable as they come and go depending on the state of the tide and even wind direction. Unless you know the area well, it's a good idea to give them a wide berth.

Buy the biggest waterproof chart case you can. You can always fold it to view just the area you are interested in. Photo: jerseykayakadventures.co.uk

USING GPS TO NAVIGATE

You should always know where you are when out paddling. If you never go out of sight of land and only go to sea in good visibility, you might think that there is little point in knowing your exact co-ordinates. However, if you get into trouble, being able to give precise co-ordinates to the coastguard is always more useful than just telling them that you are a couple of miles off a particular bay. An alternative is to provide them with a bearing and rough distance from a point, assuming you have good visibility.

Fish tend to congregate in particular spots, often referred to as marks. Although not impossible to find by conventional navigation, these marks are easier to find if you have a GPS. A handheld GPS receiver can pinpoint your position to within 30m (or often a lot better than that), saving you getting out the map and compass. You can also record your location so you can easily visit the spot again.

Another huge benefit of having a GPS is that it gives you an accurate indication of the kayak's speed. While it is always interesting to see how fast you are going, it can also be an invaluable safety aid as your kayak's drift will tell you how fast the current is flowing. This information, used in combination with the wind direction and strength, can help you decide if it is safe to anchor or not.

Standalone GPS

GPS come in two different types: standalone units and integrated GPS/sounders. If you already have a fish finder, then you may well just need a standalone GPS unit and there are a number of excellent units on the market. On small boats you'll often see a standalone GPS mounted alongside a fish finder. If you are going to go down the route of having two separate devices, I think that a fixed fish finder and a handheld GPS is the best combination, as having two fixed units on a kayak can take up a lot of space as well as a lot of battery power.

There are some compact and waterproof handheld units out there that will run for a long time on a single set of batteries. The simplest of these units are little more than a display with latitude and longitude on it, with no reference to your surroundings. Pay a little more money, and you can have a sophisticated unit that also displays chart information and displays your relative position.

This Garmin is mounted on a bracket to bring it closer, making it easier to reach.

It really is a question of how much you are prepared to pay for a handheld GPS. The top-of-the-range models can set you back £400, but for that you'll get a high sensitivity GPS receiver, an electronic compass and a barometric altimeter in a tiny device complete with its own inbuilt colour screen. You might not think you need an altimeter on a kayak, but being able to measure changes in air pressure can be very useful for weather prediction. (Weather will generally improve when pressure increases and worsen when pressure decreases.)

You can import and export data from these devices using data cards, and most of these are totally waterproof and even float. Handheld units are available which use the same quality of charts as fixed units (the latter can be far more expensive). These can be a relatively cheap way of accessing high-quality electronic charting.

Marine mounting brackets are freely available and if you attach one of these brackets to the kayak you can just slot the handheld into its mount and off you go. You can then also use the handheld for mountain biking or walking. It is worth thinking about how you are going to use your handheld, as some of the cheaper units can't have mapping added at a later stage.

Combined unit

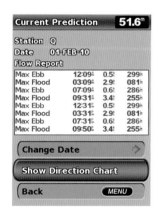

Current Prediction		51.6ᵐ

Although the combination of a handheld GPS and a standalone fish finder is a popular choice, I've now come to rely on just the one unit: a combined chart plotter, GPS unit and fish finder. Having everything in one box makes everything easy and there is one less thing to forget when I'm packing all the stuff in the car. The unit I use even has extra data loaded such as tidal streams and the times of high and low water. Having tidal data available can be a real advantage over digging out the tidal stream atlas. However, avoid the temptation to change your plan half-way through the trip simply because you can access this information while out in your kayak. You should have considered all information (e.g. strength of tidal stream) in your trip plan before getting anywhere near the water, and have told someone else of this plan.

A combined unit is obviously more expensive to buy and, if anything goes wrong, then you lose all your functions. Installing such a unit is generally easier however, as there is only a single power source required, only one battery to charge and only one screen to go wrong.

The Garmin 451 can even show the strength and direction of tidal flows.

Caution!

A word of caution must be given to those of you who might become overconfident with all the electronics is it possible to install on a kayak. Some of the stuff available to mount on a kayak is nothing short of amazing, and for £600 or so you can get enough computer power to go to the moon and back. Just because the unit is capable of taking you there and back, however, doesn't necessarily make it safe to do so.

Even the best electronics can and do fail; this is even more likely on a kayak compared to other boats. Always think about how you would get home if everything did decide to fail. Learn enough basic navigation to ensure you can always find your way home even in fog and with a broken GPS.

SEE UNDERWATER WITH A FISH FINDER

You'd be forgiven for thinking that, with a fish finder installed on your kayak, it's just a matter of paddling around until the fish show up on the screen. Drop down some bait and tea's sorted – well, not quite. The name 'fish finder' is actually a bit of a misnomer as it's really unusual for a fish finder to actually find fish. The more basic units are little more than a depth gauge, although this can be very useful. The more sophisticated units are capable of producing an astonishingly detailed picture of the sea bottom below the kayak. Some advanced units can even provide you with seabed details off to the sides.

It is quite unusual to find fish just sitting around above a featureless bottom; the chances are that a bigger fish will come along and eat them. Most fish are either hiding out somewhere, trying to avoid being eaten or waiting to ambush an unsuspecting passer-by with the intention of turning it into lunch (or both). It is these ambush and hiding spots that you use a fish finder to locate.

Perhaps the most well-known fish holding feature is manmade: the wreck. The coastline around the UK is littered with wrecks, many from the two world wars, and they make excellent fish holding features.

Standalone or combined?

My first fish finder was fitted to the Tarpon's rail system.

You have a choice of either fitting a unit that is just a fish finder (and carry a separate standalone GPS unit with you) or fit a combined unit that will serve as chart plotter, GPS and fish finder all at once.

When I started kayak fishing I was adamant I would never take any electronics afloat other than a radio. Within a couple of months, and after fishing with a number of other kayak anglers, I decided that a fish finder was quite a cool gadget but that I didn't need a GPS. I added a basic Garmin 140 fish finder to the kayak, more to act as a depth gauge than anything else. However, within a couple of months I decided I quite fancied a GPS as well.

Handheld GPS units are a great way of getting an accurate position fix.
Photo: garmin.com

Since my iPhone included basic GPS functions, I bought charting software for the iPhone and used it as a chart plotter. As the iPhone isn't waterproof it had to be kept in an Aquapack all the time, which made it hard to use. It eventually gave way to a neat little standalone GPS unit. This was great, particularly the function to tell me how fast I was going. I was still lacking in the charting department, however, and my little handheld unit had a very small screen.

The final solution for me was to go the whole hog and upgrade to a brand new shiny all-in-one unit. It has a colour screen and combines superb charts, excellent GPS and a decent sounder, all in one compact and waterproof unit.

I can only point out that kayak fishing is very addictive and, if you're likely to get the bug, fitting a combined GPS/plotter/sounder in the first place makes a lot of sense. However, it is certainly more expensive than a simple fish finder and a handheld GPS.

Fitting a battery

Some fish finders have a portable option (e.g. the portable version of the Garmin 140) which basically consists of an external weatherproof battery pack into which you can load batteries. The unit will sit on top of the battery case. Such units also come with a suction cup to attach the transducer, and can be useful if you are moving from one kayak to another or want to use your fish finder on a boat as well as a kayak. Unfortunately, the suction cup won't stick to some kayaks because the plastic surface is not smooth enough.

The vast majority of fish finders and GPS plotters will require you to fit a rechargeable 12 volt battery inside the hull of the kayak. You should use a sealed battery for obvious reasons. The size of battery which you will require depends on the current drawn by your electronics. A basic fish finder will draw a current of around 0.5 amp from a battery in an hour of constant operation. A 3 amp-hour battery should be capable of running this unit for at least six hours (long enough for the average fishing trip).

For colour fish finders, or fish finders with an inbuilt plotter, the current draw can be much higher such as 1.2 amps; a 7 amp-hour battery is probably a better bet in this case. This type of battery can be easily obtained from electrical outlets.

A sandwich box makes a cheap waterproof battery container.

Opinions vary on whether to enclose your battery in a waterproof box or not. I read an amusing thread on an American website pointing out that there is no point in enclosing your battery. According to the author, for the battery to be underwater at any point you'd have so much water in the hull of your kayak that an interruption of power to your fish finder would be the least of your problems. While that's certainly true, I like to enclose mine in a waterproof box to protect the terminals from corrosion. The box is also somewhat easier to secure within the hull than the battery alone.

I use a standard watertight sandwich box which can be obtained from the supermarket for a few pounds. The wire out from the box goes to a standard in-line automotive fuse carrier, which will blow if there is a short circuit. It exits the box via a cable gland to keep the box watertight when the lid is in place. To charge the battery, it is a simple matter of removing the battery from the box and unclipping the cable from the battery terminals.

The battery box can be secured by sticking it to the hull with a generous blob of a marine silicon sealant. If you want to be able to remove the box, Velcro can be stuck to both hull and box and then used to hold the box in place. A third method is to make a foam cut-out in the shape of the box and secure this to the hull. It's always a good idea to carry a few spare fuses with you (perhaps inside the box itself). If they are going to blow, then they will no doubt blow at the start of a promising session.

Waterproof, waterproof, waterproof

Most fish finders are made for bigger boats where they will be mounted on a console or even on the bridge. On a kayak, however, the unit is going to be mounted just a few centimetres above the sea and is quite likely to receive a regular drenching. Any unit must therefore be completely waterproof, including any plugs and sockets as these are often the parts which corrode first.

Display unit

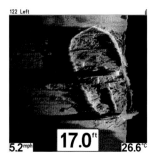

122 Left

5.2ᵐᵖʰ **17.0**ᶠᵗ 26.6°ᶜ

The display unit is available in different resolutions. More pixels mean more detail to the picture, but also that the unit uses more power. Colour can be a very useful feature but also comes at the price of a greater drain to the battery. More pixels and a colour screen can provide very impressive levels of detail. Some of the latest side-imaging fish finders are like watching a movie of the seabed below you. The shot of the wreck off Norfolk (illustrated) demonstrates the level of detail which can be obtained.

This was taken using a kayak-mounted Humminbird side-scan fish finder off Hopton.

It's amazing to think that for less than £1,000 you can buy the type of kit that just a decade ago was only available to professional wreck hunters and cost a small fortune. Nowadays, even £100 will still buy a very capable unit.

Transducer

The transducer transmits and receives the signal used to build up a picture of the seabed. Mounting the transducer in a plastic kayak can be a complicated task, as they are mainly intended for use on glass fibre boats. The exception to this is the Ocean Kayak range of kayaks and the Humminbird fish finder range, which have been made for each other. Many of the Ocean Kayak designs have pre-moulded holes into which the transducer fits. Some even have custom mountings for the display unit moulded into the hull.

A modified scupper hole in the hull makes fitting a transducer straightforward.

This ease in mounting the transducer is a huge plus point as it enables the transducer to be mounted in the water with no hull between the transducer and the water to degrade the signal. Another plus is that for units with water temperature measurement built in, you get the water temperature rather than the hull temperature.

Some Ocean Kayak Angler versions come with a dedicated fitting to take a fish finder.

Other fish finder transducers can also be fitted into the scupper holes of Ocean Kayak boats, but they might require a bit of DIY to make them fit.

Fitting the transducer

You can mount the transducer unit on some sort of arm which is fixed to the kayak and then moved into position when the kayak is afloat. There are a number of such devices available, and those kayak manufacturers that have equipped their kayaks with a rail-type mounting system will often also produce an accessory to mount the transducer in this way.

The advantage of mounting a transducer like this is that it is in direct contact with the water, for a better signal and a more accurate water temperature measurement (if included). A mounting such as this is also easy to move from kayak to kayak, or even from kayak to boat, so might prove suitable to those of us lucky enough to have more than one kayak.

The drawback of this type of arrangement is that the transducer needs to be moved out of the water when you come ashore. Otherwise, it will hit the bottom and possibly be damaged. It also adds clutter to the top of the kayak, which might catch your line.

For these reasons, most people who mount a fish finder on their kayak end up gluing the transducer to the inside of the hull, despite the poorer signal. It also means that you'll have to make a hole in your kayak to let the lead from the transducer and the battery that powers the unit from inside the hull out to where you've mounted the display unit.

The hole through which the wire from the transducer comes out of the hull will have to be sealed. While some people just drill the smallest hole possible and fill it with a suitable sealant, I like to use a marine-grade cable gland. The slight hitch here is the size of the plug on some fish finders, as this plug will have to come out through the hole and go through the gland before it can be sealed. The wire for the transducer (and the wire for the battery, if this is separate) is usually quite small, but you will need to search for a gland which is big enough for the plug or plugs to pass through but is also capable of sealing around the much smaller cables. The only way to be really sure is to take the plug along to a chandlery shop, explain the problem and get them to supply the correctly sized gland. There does seem to be a trend for plugs to get smaller on newer fish finders, so hopefully this will be less of a problem in the future.

Position the empty gland on the kayak and mark the position of the holes with a pencil.

Bolt the gland onto the hull with A4 stainless steel bolts before drilling the hole for the cable.

Fit the cable into the split rubber gasket then tighten the gland to form a waterproof seal.

There can be a temptation to cut the cable to fit it through the gland. I've seen some very neat installations where this has been done, but be aware that doing this voids any warranty on the electronics. It will also make the unit much harder to sell if you eventually decide on an upgrade or change kayaks. If you do go down this route, however, there are some very good waterproof plugs on the market.

Once you've got the transducer inside the hull and the plug on the outside, it's time to attach the transducer to the hull. Gluing the transducer is a bit of a dark art as not much tends to stick well to the plastics used to mould the vast majority of kayaks (although those of you lucky enough to have a GRP kayak will find it easy to epoxy the sensor in place).

With a plastic kayak you have a couple of options: either stick the transducer directly to the hull or create a moulding in which the transducer sits. Fill this moulding with a suitable liquid (water will do but you'll need to keep it topped up). Kits are available using a mineral oil or some people use Vaseline.

If you stick the transducer directly to the hull it's important to give the chosen spot a rub with some fine-grade sandpaper. You then need to ensure that the abraded surface is clean and free of any dust. The best way to do this is to clean the area with a rag soaked in isopropyl alcohol or white spirit, and to keep cleaning the surface of the plastic until no more colour comes off onto the rag.

Most installations that I have seen have used either a two-part epoxy marine glue or silicon-type glue. There are a couple of problems with using marine epoxy. The first is that epoxy sets hard which leaves a stiff spot in the hull. The second problem is potentially more serious: some brands of epoxy can become very hot when they are curing and even potentially hot enough to damage the hull in some cases. Be careful if using this method.

Any air bubbles in the sealant between the transducer head and the hull will result in problems with the operation of the unit. Make sure you don't have any bubbles in the mix – vigorous stirring is not recommended.

Transducers have to be mounted in the correct orientation to get the best results. Make sure you read the instructions to find out which is the front and back of the transducer and align it correctly inside the hull. Most transducers are streamlined so the pointed end is likely to be the front and the flat end the back (but check manufacturer's instructions before installing).

To fix the transducer, mark out an area on the hull slightly larger than the transducer using a long sausage of Plasticine or similar. Use the Plasticine to constrain the pool of sealant, into which you put the transducer. Press gently from back to front to settle the unit to expel any air. Place a weight on top of the transducer and leave for at least 24 hours without moving the kayak.

The sensor is bedded in with Sikaflex 291 sealant and held in place with foam wedged against the hull.

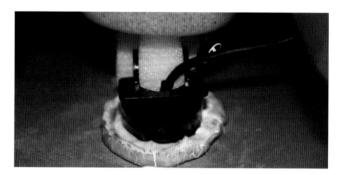

It may sound complicated, but hopefully you'll only ever have to do it once or whenever you change kayaks. A little bit of effort to get the transducer properly set up is time well spent; there is nothing worse than finding that your electronics have suddenly stopped working and the transducer is rattling around loose in your hull.

Care of your fish finder

As with other kayaking electronics, it's vital that you wash off your fish finder after use. Make sure that it isn't put away damp and salty, as this is a sure way to reduce its service life. A spray of WD40 onto the contacts will help to displace any moisture. If a blanking cap is fitted to the cable, this should be used whenever the cable is unplugged. Some people also fill the contacts with Vaseline, as this keeps out any moisture.

Fishfinder in use.
Photo: David Morris
www.anglersafloat.com

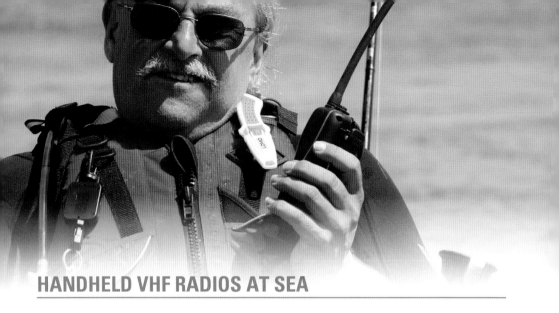

HANDHELD VHF RADIOS AT SEA

The one unit of electronics which I think every kayaker at sea should carry is a handheld VHF radio. VHF radio for maritime communications was introduced around the time of the Titanic and has been at the centre of maritime safety ever since.

The idea of VHF is that a single unit transmits to every other unit within range. This is the major difference between VHF and a mobile phone, the latter being a targeted transmission to a single intended recipient. This gives VHF a major advantage in that anyone in range will hear your broadcast and you're not going to get an answer machine when what you really want is a lifeboat. However, this is also the biggest drawback of VHF radio, as only one person can transmit on any one frequency at a time.

VHF radio bands

The frequency at which you can listen to or transmit messages is carved up into discrete bands, usually identified by a number and referred to as channels. Channel 16 is the international distress channel, so don't clog it up with unnecessary chatter. This is also the channel you'd generally use to call the coastguard before agreeing on which channel to switch to. If you are going out with a group of kayakers, its best to agree beforehand which channel you are going to use for kayak-to-kayak communication.

Most radios have a function called dual watch which enables you to keep an eye on two channels at the same time. For example, you can listen to both channel 16 for the weather and safety announcements from the coastguard and channel 8 for your friends.

Training

Icom's IC-M71 is waterproof for 30 minutes at a depth of 1.5m, and it has a long battery life. Photo: icomuk.co.uk

The whole issue of which channels to use can be a little complicated. For this reason, you have to attend a training course (another good way to meet new kayak anglers) and complete a short, mainly multiple choice, exam before you can operate a unit at sea in the UK. The government department in charge of radio at sea is the Maritime and Coastguard Agency, but they have authorised the Royal Yachting Association to issue the necessary certificate of competence. Look for RYA courses leading to the Marine Radio Short Range Certificate, often abbreviated to just SRC.

You can find training centres via the RYA website (rya.org.uk), and they are usually offered by most boat training centres as well as some adult learning centres. It pays to shop around a bit as there can be quite a variation in price. It might also be worthwhile getting together with a group of other kayakers and organising a course just for your group.

The subject of VHF radio is a complicated subject and worthy of a book in its own right. Luckily, Tim Bartlett has written the excellent *RYA VHF Handbook*. The book pretty much covers the RYA radio course and, although it's very much aimed at users of GMDSS-enabled sets, it's still packed with valuable information and should be in every kayaker's library.

Equipment licence

Once you've passed your RYA exam and proudly received your certificate through the post, you're ready to go. Well, not quite. It's not only you that needs to be licensed – you must also have a licence for the radio equipment itself.

There are two sorts of licences available. As the owner of a hand-held radio, the one you'll need is a **Ship Portable Radio Licence** (unlike the more usual **Ship Fixed Radio Licence** which covers all radios installed on a vessel). The Ofcom website is very easy to use, and it only takes a couple of minutes to fill out the details and get licensed. The licence lasts for a lifetime, although you have to tell Ofcom every ten years that you're still the licensee. While getting two bits of paper may seem like a lot of trouble, if you don't have all the required paperwork then you can be fined up to £5,000, imprisoned for almost a year and have your gear confiscated.

It's worth noting that, unlike for the Fixed Radio Licence, you'll be allocated a T-number to identify your handheld radio rather than a call sign or even an MMSI number (the latter identify ships, not individual radios). The T-number identifies the radio itself, and enables you to use the radio on any vessel. This system is set up for large ships, where portable radios are likely to be used by people such as pilots switching between ships. It doesn't make a lot of sense for kayakers, however, where the portable radio and the kayak are (hopefully) never likely to be separated.

In practice, a lot of kayakers give their kayak a name and use this as a call sign; it's unusual for people to give their T-numbers over the radio. When talking to the coastguard over the radio, it's worth telling them that you are in a kayak. Identifying yourself as 'kayak Jonah' will instantly tell the coastguard important information about your vessel. The main thing to remember is that if you are genuinely in trouble, the coastguard will be more interested in getting help to you than telling you off for not knowing your T-number.

Don't be afraid to use your radio. When you've finished your course it pays to practise by talking to friends, requesting radio checks when you go out and generally getting used to using the radio. If you ever do need to make an emergency call, things will go smoother if you're comfortable with your particular set.

Going Digital

When you do your radio course you'll be introduced to a system known as Digital Selective Calling (DSC). DSC automates a lot of the calling operations carried out on channel 16, and enables the radio to talk to a boat's GPS and transmit the position of the vessel along with a distress call. It also gives each ship a unique identifying number, or Maritime Mobile Service Identity (MMSI).

Before you leave your RYA course full of excitement for the new system, it currently only applies to radios fitted to larger vessels and isn't yet available for handheld units. The reason for this is that there is no international agreement on how to implement these extra functions in a handheld unit. As a result, there is no agreed standard for a handheld VHF DSC unit to be compared with. No such unit can therefore be licensed for use in the UK.

There are ongoing international efforts to overcome these problems; hopefully handheld DSC sets will be available at some point in the not-too-distant future. Confusingly, you may see units imported into the UK promising this functionality; they can't be used in the UK, however. For this reason, be careful when buying radios from websites or boat jumbles. You might discover that a perfectly serviceable unit is actually illegal in the UK because it hasn't yet been type approved. The type approval mark has to be displayed on the unit, in the form of the well known CE mark, so if this is missing from a unit, chances are it hasn't got type approval and you should find out why before you buy it.

Buying a radio

Icom's IC-M33 is a good radio, which also floats if you drop it in the water.

Photo: icomuk.co.uk

The main thing to look for when buying a radio is how waterproof it is. Your radio will be drenched with seawater on a regular basis, so the more waterproof and corrosion resistant the better. An ingress protection (IP) rating is used to measure how waterproof a radio is. This consists of two digits, where the first measures a radio's protection against the ingress of dust (which isn't usually a problem for us). The value of the second, more relevant, digit is what is important to us. An IP rating of X7 is probably the lowest you should consider (unless you are prepared to carry your radio around in a sealed bag or dry sack); this should be waterproof for 30 minutes immersion to a depth of 1m.

It is worth noting that a radio with a decent IP rating still needs maintenance. It's really important to get rid of any seawater on the unit when you get home, and make sure that the battery contacts are dry before you put it on charge.

There are also radios on the market which float and I must admit to having purchased one when they came out. It's been to sea with me quite a few times but since it's always leashed to my PFD, I've never once dropped it over the side. I'm not exactly sure how worthwhile this facility is in the first place, and would perhaps forego the floating property for better corrosion resistance or waterproofing.

Another thing to look for in a portable radio is the power output – most are around 5 watts although some 6 watt models are available. The law constrains VHF radios to a maximum output of 25 watts, but as far as I'm aware 6 Watts is the maximum available on a handheld and there is a trade-off between power and battery life.

Radio horizon

Power is not the most limiting factor in estimating the range of your handheld. The height of the antennae above the horizon determines how far away your signal will be received. VHF radio waves travel in straight lines, and don't tend to bounce off the atmosphere. In a kayak your antenna is unlikely to be more than a metre above the sea. As the range of a radio in nautical miles is limited to roughly three times the square-root of the height of the antennae in metres, the radio horizon of a handheld on a kayak will be around three nautical miles. For two kayaks to talk to each other their radio horizons must overlap, so they must be within six nautical miles of each other.

As most yachts have an aerial at the top of their masts, they can often hear you at far greater distances than your fellow kayakers.

Although this might seem a little disappointing, remember that the coastguard has a very high aerial (and loads more power). Since the range of coastguard radio is around 30 miles or more, you should be able to at least hear the coastguard almost any-where you are likely to end up fishing. But just because you can hear the coastguard, this doesn't necessarily mean that they can hear you.

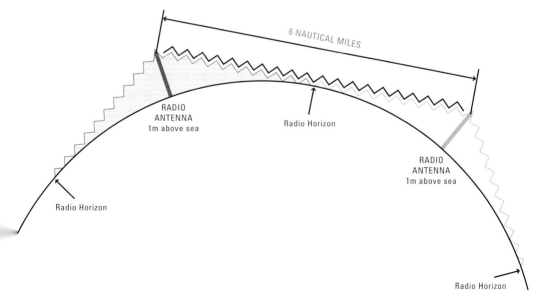

6 NAUTICAL MILES

RADIO ANTENNA
1m above sea

Radio Horizon

RADIO ANTENNA
1m above sea

Radio Horizon

Radio Horizon

FISHING SKILLS

Anchoring may well be the most dangerous part of the sport – when you are most likely to capsize, become tangled or fall off of your kayak. The golden rule of anchoring is that if you are in any doubt about the conditions, don't anchor. If the tide is ripping through, think long and hard about your level of skill and look for a less challenging spot to fish.

Once you have mastered paddling and anchoring, the other skills you're going to need to fish from a kayak are relatively few. The vast majority of your fishing will be done using just one technique: **downtiding** – running bait behind the kayak with the tide. You may also have heard of **uptiding** where the bait is cast uptide of the boat and a bow allowed to form in the line. This method isn't really relevant to kayak angling, as you are unlikely to anchor anywhere with enough tide for successful uptiding.

Anchoring

Although it's perfectly possible to fish from a drifting kayak, and this is by far the best way to fish for some species, there will come a time when you decide you want to stop somewhere and fish a particular area. You then have a couple of choices: either find something like a pot buoy to which you can secure your kayak or attach yourself to a fixed point on the seabed using an anchor.

The carabiner and anchor trolley allows the kayak to be safely anchored by the stern.

Some kayaks come with an anchor and warp, and some even have a cleat to attach the anchor warp to the kayak. Before you try to anchor for the first time, it's worth having a think about what you are trying to do. If you were anchoring a boat, you would have access to the bow and be able to retrieve an anchor from the front as well as anchor the boat with the bow into the wind or tide. The problem with a kayak is that you haven't got access to the bow, either to tie off the anchor or to retrieve it once it's down.

If you just chuck an anchor over the side and hang onto the rope it will pull your kayak side-on to the tide. This is a position you really don't want to be in as it can lead to water coming over the gunwhale. If the rope gets under the boat, it can generate quite a strong tipping action and you may end up going for a swim. This can turn into a bigger problem if you are not attached to the kayak, as you will quickly drift away from it. When anchoring in any kind of tide, a safety leash is strongly recommended to keep you attached to the kayak should the worst happen.

Anchor trolley

An anchor trolley is a device to enable you to move the anchor warp from your side, where you can reach it, to either the bow or the stern of the kayak for retrieval and anchoring. It takes the form of a pair of pulleys, one at either end of the trolley, attached either directly to the kayak or by a short length of bungee cord. The trolley can either run the full length of the kayak from bow to stern, or some people prefer a half-trolley either at the bow or stern.

The advantage of a half-trolley is that the anchor trolley lines don't cross the cockpit of the boat, which can be a problem with some designs of kayak. Some anglers go as far as to fit two half-trolleys, one at the stern and one at the bow. I've even seen some anglers with a full-length anchor trolley down both sides of the boat. This gives a massive degree of flexibility but does load your kayak up with a lot of gear.

When rigging an anchor trolley it's important to get it as close to the stern as possible.

The stability of the kayak at anchor increases as the anchor trolley's point of attachment approaches either the stern or bow. Some illustrations of US anchor trolleys show the trolley attached quite a long way from the bow or stern. While this is ok for anchoring in very sheltered waters, you want the trolley as far forward/aft as possible when anchoring in any degree of tide. Many anglers, if fishing in a kayak without a rudder, use the rudder mounting fittings that are moulded into most kayaks to attach the trolley.

Some even go as far as to create custom brackets to attach the anchor trolley.

The trolley itself consists of a loop of cord running between the two pulleys and a carabiner to attach the anchor warp. The carabiner can simply be used to connect one end of the loop to the other. However, it is better to tie one end of your anchor trolley to a stainless steel ring and the other to the carabiner, and then clip the carabiner to the ring. If the ring is fitted to the rear-facing end of the trolley and the carabineer to the forward-facing end, you can then unclip the trolley and use the carabiner as a tow line or to pull your kayak behind you if wading in shallow water. The ring will then jam in the rear block and you will have a kayak's length of line by which to tow the kayak.

A short length of bungee cord can act as a shock absorber.

Most of my fishing is done with the kayak anchored by the stern, as I like to look where I'm fishing and because my kayak sits very well when anchored this way. If you are going to be doing a lot of uptiding or your kayak is skittish when anchored by the stern, you may also wish to anchor by the bow. I prefer to recover my anchor over the bow, as my kayak has more buoyancy at that end. I use a full-length trolley so that I can transfer the anchoring point from stern to bow when it is time to pick up the anchor.

One problem that can occur with anchor trolleys is that, because they run through a couple of pulleys, they can slip. When I started out there were a couple of times when I was anchored from the stern and felt the motion of the kayak becoming more violent. When looking behind me, I noticed that the anchor trolley carabiner had moved a couple of feet back from the stern, which was enough to make the kayak quite unstable.

The answer is to fit some means of locking off the trolley. I ended up riveting a clam cleat to the side of the kayak. When I wanted to lock off the trolley I simply dropped the trolley rope into the clam cleat, which holds it fast. It's worth noting that there are both port and starboard clam cleats, so make sure you buy the right one. They only hold the rope when pulled in the right direction (pulling in the other direction will release the rope). I use the fine line versions for lines of 6mm or smaller. These are known as CL214 or CL213 cleats, depending on which side of the boat they are intended for.

This type of cleat is useful for making sure that the anchor trolley doesn't creep back towards the centre of the kayak. They are easy to rivet to the hull.

Types of anchor

Once you've got the anchor trolley rigged, it's time to look at the anchor itself. Most kayak anglers use a 1.5kg folding anchor, available quite cheaply from most chandlers. Although some like to use a lighter anchor, I prefer the 1.5kg as I've seen lighter anchors drag.

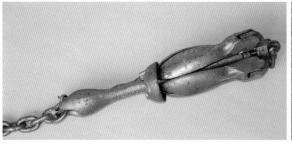

The other type of anchor you may come across is the sea anchor or drogue. This is basically a small parachute-type device which is used to slow the drift of the kayak, provided that the drift is being caused by the wind and not by the current. Drogues are deployed off the anchor trolley, and can be really useful for drift fishing.

Attaching the anchor

Although there are different opinions about this, I always attach my anchor to at least a metre of chain for a couple of reasons. The first is that warps fitted directly to the anchor can be damaged and even cut by sharp objects on the seabed. The other reason is to do with the angle at which the warp leaves the anchor. With a length of chain the warp lies flat along the seabed, and any force applied to the anchor will try to pull it along the seabed and will meet maximum resistance. With just rope, some of the force can lift the anchor which means it starts to drag. Dragging your anchor can be a good way of losing it, as it will eventually find something to become snagged on.

How you attach the chain to the anchor can also be important if you do get snagged up. When you buy the anchor, it will probably have an inviting shackle at one end which might look like the obvious place to attach the chain. However, you'll also see a loop at the nose and it is here that I attach my chain, moving the shackle and attaching it to the 'wrong' end. I then run the chain back up the shaft of the anchor, and attach it to the eye with a small cable tie. This enables the anchor to hold properly but, if it gets stuck, a good pull on the rope will break the cable tie. The anchor can then be reversed out of the snag.

You may need to play around with different cable ties to find one which breaks out at the right force, or you can make a slight nick in one with a pair of pliers. I also carry a few spare cable ties with me so that, if I have to break out an anchor, I can reset the trip and go off and fish somewhere else.

An anchor with a bulbous stem is particularly good, as the locking collar is captive and can't be lost. Note the orange cable tie.

The other way of attaching an anchor is to use a bridle, which is just a relatively short loop of rope running from one end of the anchor to the other. You then run this rope through the bottom link of the chain. When anchored up, the chain will tend to go to the rear of the loop and the anchor will hold fast. When you want to break the anchor out, simply paddle up-tide of the anchor. The chain will run up the bridle when you pull it, and the anchor can be pulled out nose first. The only slight drawback with this method is that if you have anchored in a strong tide which has then dropped off, the bridle can self-trip.

Anchor warps
With the chain attached to the anchor, it's time to think about warps. Anchoring is not an exact science, but you should think

about using around three times the depth to anchor in fairly benign conditions. If the current is ripping through, you should use around five times the depth or more (although you should consider not anchoring if it's going to be really difficult to hold).

Most of the time I'll probably be anchoring in around 20m so, for most of my fishing, 100m of warp should be enough. I always go for the thinnest warp I can get away with, which means that most of my anchoring is done with 2mm thick warp. With a breaking strain of around 85kg, this type of warp should hold almost anything; the thinner the warp the less drag and the less weight. Paracord of 3mm thickness is also a popular choice and is available in long lengths at a reasonable cost. Make sure that what you buy is a single continuous length; sometimes you can end up with a couple of lengths loosely joined. You don't want to discover this by losing an anchor, so run it though your hands before you first use it.

Some ropes come on a card which can be used as a winder. If you are only going to anchor occasionally, in shallow water, then this might be all you need. However, the popular option is to use a divers' surface marker buoy (SMB) reel, commonly used to deploy a surface marker buoy above divers on the bottom. These make a very neat job of storing the warp, and most have stainless steel fittings so they won't rust. Some even come with 100m of 3mm warp, making them a very cost-effective solution.

A dive reel makes a good anchor reel; this one holds 100m of 3mm line.

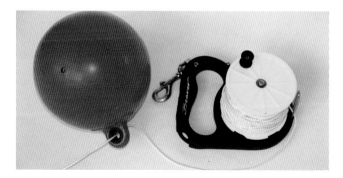

Once the anchor and chain are safely on the bottom, the divers' reel is effectively anchored to the bottom. To anchor up, all you need to do is run the anchor warp through your carabiner, run the carabiner to either the bow or stern and attach the dive reel to the kayak. It's always worth leaving a few metres of rope on the dive reel. This will allow you to reposition your kayak if you are over a particularly rough bit of ground and will also to give you a bit of slack to let out when it's time to recover the anchor.

Quick-release system

Many people are quite happy to just clip the dive reel onto the kayak. There is another way of fitting an anchor, however, which gives you a little more flexibility. This involves attaching a small buoy and a further length of rope, which together make a quick-release system. By having a small buoy running freely along the anchor warp (before the dive reel), you can put the anchor down and then have the dive reel floating at the surface, held up by the buoy.

You can then have 3–4m of floating rope attached to the dive reel with a carabiner, which you can use to effectively moor the kayak to your dive reel much as you would to a pot buoy or other mooring point. This has the advantage that the buoy then takes the weight of the warp rather than your kayak. You can then run the rope from the buoy to your kayak via the carabiner on your anchor trolley, and secure the rope to your kayak. If you use a cam-type cleat, then the rope can be wedged in the cleat to anchor. If you need to get away in a hurry, either to take a photo of a mate's fish or for safety reasons, you can just free the rope from the cleat and you are free. You can then come back and pick up the buoy, with your anchor attached, whenever you want to.

The so-called quick-release system also has the advantage that, if the anchor becomes snagged and you can't break it out, you can leave the anchor and buoy and come back later to recover it. Another advantage of this system is that it provides you with a

length of floating rope with a carabiner at one end which can be used for other purposes (for example, to moor up to pot buoys or for tying off to another kayak).

Recovering your anchor

I nearly always recover my anchor from the front of the kayak, because this is where the hull has most buoyancy. If I'm anchored by the stern then the first step is to let go of the quick-release system, which leaves the kayak drifting down-tide of the marker buoy with the rope streaming out behind the buoy. I then bring the carabiner to the middle of the anchor trolley and paddle up to the buoy. I grab hold of the buoy and release the clutch on the diver's reel so that the line starts to pay out and the kayak drifts backwards once any forward momentum has dissipated. While the line is slack I put it through the carabiner, lock off the reel and run the trolley up to the bow. I then put the trolley line through a locking cleat to keep the carabiner at the bow. The kayak is then anchored from the bow and the anchor can be pulled up and in. Once the chain has reached the carabiner, it's a simple matter of bringing the dive reel back to the side of the kayak and taking it out of the carabiner.

It's worth practising anchoring a few times in sheltered waters, and making sure that you can easily get the anchor back on board. If you think you are going to have a problem getting the anchor back, then don't anchor in the first place.

When pulling up my anchor I always mentally go through the process step-by-step before starting it for real. This helps me to ensure that I do everything in the right order. It is always a good idea to fish with other more experienced kayakers. Ask someone to show you their anchor set-up and demonstrate it so you can see how the process works.

Downtiding

If you are already a boat fisherman then the chances are that you'll already have the vast majority of the gear that you're going to need to fish from a kayak. If you are just starting out then you don't need very much gear: a couple of rods and reels, a few lures and a relatively small amount of terminal tackle. Even if you go for relatively high-end tackle, it shouldn't cost you much more than £300–400 to set yourself up. If you want to use starter equipment from the bottom end of the market, you might only spend as little as £100.

I use this type of leash for my rods, as the quick release makes it easy to detach when you get a bite.

Types of rod

Opinions vary here, and you often see very short rods sold as kayaking rods. While these are easy to control on a kayak, I prefer to use something a little longer. The defining length for me is the distance from my seat to the bow of the kayak, so that if a fish runs across the bow I can guide the line round without it being fouled on the bow. For my kayak, this means a rod length of about seven feet.

When it comes to rod strengths I have always preferred to fish light. On a kayak, not only does light gear give you more sport, but a lighter rod will also cushion any sudden runs from a fish. If using a thick heavy rod, a sudden run might unbalance you.

For most of my fishing I use a 6lb class boat rod, and hardly ever have to use more than three ounces of lead (I often fish with one ounce or less). If I'm after bigger fish, such as conger or tope, I will switch to a soft-actioned 12–20lb class rod.

Types of reel

Choice of reel is also personal. Kayak fishing doesn't require much from a reel except for excellent corrosion resistance. I don't bother with much in the way of breaking and go for a basic model with a level wind. Brand-name reels like Penn, Shimano, Daiwa or Abu should all be up to the job. For lighter work I use an Abu 6500, but a Penn 320 or a Daiwa Slosh would also be a good choice. For heavier lines I use Shimano Calcutta 700s but an Abu 7000, or one of the larger Penn boat multipliers would also work well.

(Left) here's an Abu 6500 on a rod in a RAM mount, safely constrained by a leash. (Right) I use this Shimano Calcutta 700 for my heavier kayak fishing.

I've not had any problems with corrosion on the reels as yet, but I do religiously wash them in freshwater after every trip. I find that the smaller reels in particular need stripping and greasing once every three months or so to keep them in tip-top condition.

Tackle

Kayak angling is very hard on tackle because it is so close to salt water. You have the choice of either investing in good-quality gear and looking after it well, or go for cheaper stuff which you would then replace every season or so. Part of your decision will come down to how religiously you use a rod leash. If you don't leash your tackle you will lose it, and at that point you may be glad you only bought a cheap reel!

In keeping with using lighter fishing tackle, I only use braided lines on a kayak. I prefer the non-stretch type of line and a thinner diameter; this means you can get away with far less lead than with conventional lines.

WHAT TO FISH FOR

An odd looking gurnard. Just in front of the pectoral fin on each side are three spiny legs which it uses to stir up food off the bottom.

How you fish from your kayak will depend to a large extent on how much time you've got available for fishing and how seriously you want to take it. Your kayak is amazingly portable, and you can quite literally follow the fish around the country. I know anglers who think nothing of driving hundreds of miles to fish. If catching fish is your main motivation, then there are definitely certain times of the year and certain places that will yield the best results. Following the fish around can be great fun – you can meet new people and try new spots at the same time. You may even find that the change of scenery and the chance to explore different places is just as interesting as the fishing.

If you fancy this kind of fishing then it is worth signing up to some of the angling/kayaking websites and reading the angling press; you'll soon start to get an idea of what can be caught where. Most kayak angling websites have a 'Let's meet' section. Some organise regular trips around the country, which gives you a chance to fish new areas in the company of accomplished kayakers (great from a safety point of view). There are a growing number of localised kayak fishing websites springing up, which are great for detailed knowledge about specific areas. In some areas, there are even kayak angling clubs which are growing from strength to strength.

For most people, however, it's probably more a case of having to fish locally and catch whatever is out there on the day (and very good fun this type of fishing can be too). This chapter looks at some of the fish you are most likely to catch and the methods that work best to catch them.

Mackerel

I always feel rather sorry for the poor old mackerel. Although amazingly tasty to eat, very good for you and great sport, the mackerel is just too easy to catch and hence often overlooked. This is a shame, as it's probably the first fish you are likely to catch on a kayak. It will also provide you with great fun, as well as a vast supply of free bait for which to catch all sorts of other species.

Fly caught mackerel.
Photo: David Morris
www.anglersafloat.co.uk

The mackerel is a seasonal visitor to our waters, and turns up for the warmer months when you are most likely to be taking your first steps afloat. Huge shoals of mackerel spread up the English Channel and gradually spread out around our coasts, even making their way as far north as Scotland. Although the shoals are not as vast as when they supported massive fishing industries right around the coast, they are still relatively plentiful.

How to catch mackerel

The mackerel is a voracious feeder, living on just about anything smaller than itself which is too slow to get away. Because they hang around in vast shoals, the first one to see a meal has to eat it as quickly as possible before another gets in there. This is the behaviour exploited to catch them, and the most usual method is a string of feathers. Named after the feather that was used to make them in times gone by, feathers are very closely related to the fly anglers' fly, and are an imitation bait fish. Feathers are nearly always used in sets of three or more, known as a string.

Feathers consist of a sharp hook with something coming off the hook to resemble the mackerels' main prey. Although feathers are still used, you are more likely nowadays to see bits of plastic, tinsel or luminous beads. The latter gives the imitation fish a bit of a head, and is known as a Hokkai.

When they are feeding you can catch a lot of mackerel, sometimes more than one at a time. It's not unusual to see shore anglers pulling mackerel in six at a time from the breakwaters and piers of the southern coast. Unfortunately, many of these fish are left to rot on the quayside – a sad end for such a plucky little fish. Using six feathers is a little greedy and also a little dangerous; a full string of six wriggling around on a kayak is a sure recipe for a hook in your hand and a long, painful paddle home. It is far better to use at most a string of three, which also allows the fish to put up more of a fight.

At the risk of losing all fishing credibility, I have to admit that there are many summer evenings when I go out mackerel fishing using ultra-light tackle and just a single feather or a very small lure. On this balanced tackle, a single large mackerel can give an amazing account of itself. To me, this sums up what kayak fishing is all about: light lines, minimal tackle and a couple of fish for the BBQ.

Mackerel as bait

Mackerel is often overlooked as an eating fish, perhaps because it is so common. As bait to catch other fish mackerel is really popular. In the summer months, and particularly down south, mackerel are so plentiful that you can rely on catching a few every time you go out which gives you a ready supply of bait. There are very few fish that won't accept a bit of fresh mackerel. The fresher the bait the better, and a strip of fresh mackerel will by far out-fish older offerings from the fishmonger or frozen fish from the supermarket (both of these can provide a good stand-by in the winter when mackerel are harder to come by).

Bass

I have to admit to a degree of bias here because bass are by far my favourite fish and the fish that got me into kayak fishing in the first place. There are a massive range of ways to fish for them from fly fishing to artificial lures and plugs, and a huge array of baits (both dead and alive).

Even small bass, known as schoolies, can be great fun on light tackle.

Using plugs and lures

My favourite method of catching bass is by imitation bait fish called plugs. These come in a massive range of shapes and sizes, and are designed to fish different sections of the water table.

Most lure anglers in the UK will fish lures using the combination of a fixed spool reel and a braided line, rather than the traditional monofilament. Although far more expensive to buy, braid is a lot thinner for a given breaking strain and, more importantly, has almost no stretch so any movement of the rod is imparted directly to the lure. Although a lot of American anglers use small bait-casting multiplier reels for lure fishing, I find I can cast further with a fixed spool reel. Using one on a kayak where it will be regularly doused in salt water does mean that you will have to invest in a decent reel in the first place. Cheap freshwater fixed spool reels don't tend to last very long on a kayak.

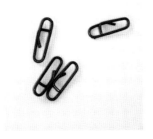

The only drawback with braid is that, because it has virtually no stretch, it can be a little unforgiving. People can lose fish when close to the kayak. For this reason, it has become common practice to add a couple of metres or so of fluorocarbon line to give you a bit of a buffer. Fluorocarbon is another relatively new line material, claimed to have a refractive index close to that of water and therefore to be almost invisible underwater. I have to admit, whatever the science, it seems to catch more fish and I now use fluorocarbon line for all my bass traces (both lure and bait).

You can connect heavier lures using a Spin Link.

Attaching the lure to the fluorocarbon is a matter of choice. For smaller lighter lures, then any form of connector can result in a detrimental effect on the action of the lure. These are best tied on directly, even although this does make changing lures more difficult. For bigger lures, Breakaway Tackle produces a clip known as a Spin Link, which does a very good job and enables you to easily change lures.

Hard lures

When it comes to the choice of lure, I think the most exciting are those that are designed to be fished at the very surface. They are cast out and retrieved, making a large commotion on the surface. This fools the bass into thinking that a wounded bait fish is up there just right for lunch. To really get the best out of this type of lure, you'll need a slightly stiffer rod than you would use for other types of lure; to work at their best, they need to be given more action. They are among the most exciting of lures because you often see the fish come up behind the lure and hit it, almost ripping the rod out of your arms. Once you've experienced this you'll find it hard to fish for other species!

Surface lures can be deadly, and fish will come up from a surprising depth to take them.

The range of lures changes every year, but a lot of them are designed to catch fishermen rather than the fish themselves. I usually just stick to a couple of designs and only try out new ones if I hear of other people consistently catching on them. Otherwise, you could easily spend a small fortune on lures and end up using just a couple of them. Unfortunately many lures have rather silly names, so you may well end up having to go into a shop and ask for a Yo Zuri Mag Popper or a Duel Aile Mag Slider. The results will be well worth it, however.

One of the huge advantages of surface lures is that they can be cast over ground that would instantly eat up a deeper diving lure. You've also got a fair chance of getting the lure, and any resultant fish, back to the kayak. However, it's not just shallow snaggy ground that can be covered with these lures. I've had fish come up from surprising depths to nail these lures, so don't always cast towards the shore and seabed features. Lures are well worth trying out on the surface even when you are quite a long way out and over a fair depth of water.

A kayak is an almost perfect platform for fishing with surface lures as you can really sneak up on the fish. Without the sound of an engine or footsteps to disturb the fish, you can get amazingly close. In addition, because you are sitting down in a kayak there is less chance of casting a shadow and spooking the fish – which can often happen when stalking fish from the shore. Every once in a while you'll get really lucky and be afloat on a balmy summer evening when the bass come to the surface to chase bait fish, causing the water to appear to boil. Cast a popper out across the boiling water and see it snatched by an eager bass: this is the kind of moment that will stay with you for a long time.

The next class of lures runs just slightly deeper than the surface type of lure and is known as the subsurface lure. These are lures designed to work the top foot or so of water. Although a relatively new phenomenon, they have proved to be quite deadly. Indeed, most of my lure fishing nowadays is carried out with one of this type of lure. Lures such as the Maria Angel Kiss and the Maria Chase BW will fish the top foot and float on the surface until you start to retrieve. You can vary the depth to which the lure will dive by varying the speed of the retrieve.

The next set of lures I regularly use for bass are one of the oldest types around. Even as a child (which is longer ago than I care to remember) I was aware of Rapala's amazing J13 and J11 lures. These swim a lot deeper than the newer subsurface lures, sometimes running down to 4m or even deeper. They can be absolutely deadly trolled behind a moving kayak; indeed, they are the only type of lures that I would use for this purpose. When you're trolling lures you might be worried about detecting a bite since, with most kayaks, the rods will be sticking out behind you. One of the first pieces of advice I was given about kayak fishing by an old hand is still very true: "you know you've got a bite when the kayak stops".

Soft lures

The most common soft lure used to be the Red Gill plastic sandeel; this does what it says on the tin and has been around for years. Recently, however, the market has exploded and there is now a vast array of gaily coloured pieces of plastic available. These range from the more obviously fish shaped to some quite outrageous-looking gaudy coloured forms that are massively removed from anything created by good old mother nature.

I tend to fish all my imitation plastic lures in much the same way: with a long or very long fluorocarbon trace and as little weight as possible. Some lures are now available where the weight and hook are combined in what is known as a lead head. I've had great success with these, combining them with lifelike imitation sand-eels. Another recent newcomer is the SlugGo, where the hook and lead are encased inside the body of the lure which makes them very good for fishing over snaggy ground. The hook point comes through the body of the lure when it's taken by a fish.

Imitation rubber eels can be very effective; this one is rigged on a lead head.

Sidewinder imitation eels can work a treat – my favourite is the white eel.

Another recent newcomer in this area is the weighted plastic lure, of which the Sidewinder sandeel imitation is probably the best known. By placing the weight inside the body of the lure, terminal tackle is massively simplified. I simply attach the lure directly to a fluorocarbon leader. Sidewinders, particularly the white-bodied variety, have proven to be very successful for bass fishing. They work very well when drifted across a known hotspot such as the top of a sandbank.

This is probably the area where things are changing most at the moment in bass fishing. New plastic lures become available almost every year, so keep reading the angling press and websites to see what is catching in your area.

Live sandeels

Most of the hard and soft lures mentioned above try to imitate a bait fish, so it should come as no surprise that using a livebait is also a very effective way to fish for bass. The most common form of livebait for bass fishing is the sandeel. Some of the southwest ports have dealers who sell live sandeels. Some tackle shops are now setting up tanks, so a supply is becoming easier to find.

Transporting and caring for live eels is a difficult job, as they need cool seawater and a lot of aeration if they are to survive. Custom bait buckets with battery-powered air pumps are available, which can keep the eels alive for several hours. Another method is to soak an old towel in seawater and then place a layer of towel, a few eels, another layer of towel, another few eels and so on into a cool box along with a few ice packs.

This bait bucket has a built-in air pump and can keep sandeels alive for several hours.

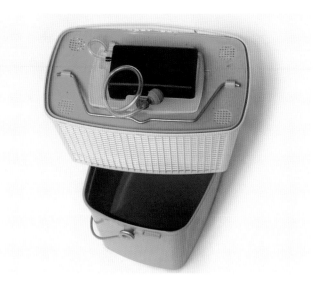

Once you've got the eels and your kayak to where you want to fish things become a little easier. Creels are widely available for sandeels, which are basically a bucket with a fine grid and holes so that seawater can circulate through the bucket. This will keep eels alive almost indefinitely. For those of you that like gadgets, a search of US websites for livebait tank designs can throw up some fascinating results. I'm not completely convinced of the merits of a livebait tank for a kayak when a creel does the job perfectly well, however.

Bait hooking a sandeel up through the mouth.

Sandeels work best as a bait when used with the bare minimum of weight. They are also very effective if used with no weight at all, a method known as freelining. Use a large hook, such as a 4/0 Kamasan B940, and a long fluorocarbon trace. Drifting a freelined eel along with the kayak can be very effective.

Bass are quite voracious feeders and it's not just sandeels that will be taken. If they get the chance, bass will also take a small live mackerel, pout whiting and indeed just about anything that is small enough for them to get into their mouths.

Traditional bait

Crab or worm are a more traditional bait for bass. Peeler crabs are widely recommended to be the best bait after a live sandeel. These are best collected yourself at low water, although they can be bought at some tackle shops. The small green shore crabs are very good, but if you can get hold of some velvet swimming crabs these are even better. Baiting up with crab requires the use of a hook with a wider gape than normal to keep the point of the hook clear of the crab. The bait is whipped onto the hook shank with a thin elastic to keep it in place.

Bass will also take worm baits, although it has to be said that most often worms will catch the smaller fish (or schoolies). Both lug and rag worm work, and your choice should depend on venue. Rag might be completely useless at one place while it may be the only worm worth fishing at another; local knowledge is important.

Fly fishing

The final method of bass fishing, and one which is growing at a rate of knots, is fly fishing. In the US, it is considered to be rather poor form to cast sitting down in a kayak. Common sense seems to have prevailed and in the UK you very seldom see people standing in a kayak. You can cast over a good distance sitting down and our waters are slightly rougher than the Florida Everglades. One thing to consider here is that salt water will rapidly destroy a lot of fly gear intended for trout fishing, including some of the lines. Look out for gear that is intended for salt water use and make sure that everything is washed down thoroughly before being put away.

Fly fishing is actually just a variation of lure fishing. The main difference is that you don't use the weight of the lure to cast it out, but rather rely on the action of the line. Again, as with hard lures, you can buy lures to fish various areas of the water. Chose between a floating, an intermediate or a sinking line, and use this to control whether you fish at the surface or slightly deeper. Whatever choice of line you make, it's worth using a fluorocarbon leader.

Bass flies tend to be somewhat bigger than the equivalent flies used for trout. As a result, you'll need a beefier rod to cast them any distance. A #8 or #9 rod is ideal, and an eight foot length can be handled in a kayak without having to resort to standing. Don't forget to add a lot of backing (preferably braid) as a decent bass is capable of taking a lot of line off a fly angler so be prepared.

Fly fishing is certainly becoming popular with kayak anglers. The combination of fly fishing and kayaking has a certain perfection to it; a warm summer evening and a shoal of fish feeding on the surface can make for some absolutely amazing fly fishing. Once you've experienced it, you might even find that using a traditional rod and line is a little dull.

Bass nursery areas

Bass fishing is probably the closest thing we have to the type of sport fishing enjoyed in the US. We are just beginning to take this side of things seriously, with both size limits for the fish you can take home and some 37 nursery areas where you can't fish for bass from a boat (to protect the younger year classes of fish). The size limit for bass is 36cm, although there is pressure for this to be increased. Any fish which measures less than 36cm must be returned immediately. There is a growing trend in bass fishing towards catch and release in general and not just with the smaller fish. As the bigger fish are more likely to breed, it makes sense to put the big ones back as well to help protect future stocks. Details of bass nursery areas and any local rules which apply can be found on the UKBass.com website.

Conger

Conger eels, one of the bigger fish you are likely to encounter, can be great fun to catch from a kayak. The numbers of conger around our coasts seems to have increased in recent years, with eels moving into rough ground quite close to shore and becoming caught quite regularly even by shore anglers.

Now all he has to do is get the conger off the hook!.

Congers just love rough ground and like to live in holes – wartime wrecks are a real conger favourite. The problem with fishing for congers is that, once they've taken bait, they try to get back to their hole. If you let the eel get back in, the chances are you won't ever get it out again. Congering tackle tends to be fairly heavy weight compared to most gear you'll use on a kayak, so you can get stuck into the fish right from the start. Note that congers also have very sharp teeth and can cut though lighter mono. Anglers used to use wire traces for congering, but more recently there has been a tendency towards heavy mono hook lengths. A common breaking strain is 200lb if you are targeting the bigger eels. In terms of line, I like to use a 30lb braid which gives me enough leverage to ensure I get the fish away from the bottom quickly.

Congers are big-time predators and like nothing better than a fish bait. A whole mackerel can work well and a mackerel flapper, in which the tail and backbone are removed to leave just two fillets attached to the head, can be even better. Squid can also be an effective bait.

Pollock

From a culinary point of view, pollock used to be a much under-rated fish. They have started to be promoted by the trendier chefs, so perhaps the times are changing. Pollock are very much an ambush predator, and will be found hanging out wherever there is decent cover. Wrecks, very rough ground and kelp beds are good places to start looking for them. These fish are very plentiful in the southwest, and will probably be the next thing you catch after a mackerel. As tiny fish, they move inshore in massive shoals in the summer.

Pollock are famous for crash diving when they take a bait. You'll always know when you've got one on the end of the line, and that first run is exhilarating.

As voracious predators, pollock will often resort to the same tactics

as bass. Rubber eels are a firm favourite, and some will even end up taking feathers. The classic pollock rig is a jelly worm, fished on a long trace held away from the main line and lead by a tube boom. Red jelly worms with black tails seem to work amazingly well for me and far outfish other colour combinations. Fly fishing tactics can also work well for pollock, particularly when the fish come up in the water chasing small fry on a summer evening.

Flatfish

The flounder is a much underrated fish and one which, in the depths of winter, can still be relied upon to give the dedicated angler a bit of excitement. Flounder are famous for inhabiting estuary systems, particularly those in the south of the country. The estuaries of the southwest, such as the Teign, were once famous for their winter flounder fishing. The commercial removal of the fish for pot baits has greatly reduced numbers, however, although there are always rumours of a comeback.

Flounders tend to become fixated on one type of food, and this changes from estuary to estuary. Fishing Poole harbour with peeler crab is probably a complete waste of time, as the fish there are almost all caught on small rag worm. A little further down the coast in the Teign estuary, however, the fish are caught almost exclusively on peeler crab. It really pays to get to know some local anglers. Look out for the results of local fishing matches – not only will this tell you where the fish are being caught, but it may also give you some indication of what bait to use.

A Poole harbour flounder from the south coast.

Flounders are like the magpies of the aquatic world, and are often drawn to shiny beads or sequins used by anglers above their hooks. Indeed, anglers used to fish for flounder using flounder spoons (the head of a spoon cut from the handle and fitted above the hook). When twitched over the seabed, the flounder will come to see what's happening. The more modern version of plastic spoons are still used, but dayglo beads have largely taken their place.

It may sound strange to suggest float fishing for something that is obviously a bottom-dwelling fish, but this can be a very good method in the shallower estuaries. This also allows the angler to use far lighter gear, which in turn enables the flounder to give a better account of itself.

There are many other flatfish that you may be lucky enough to catch, ranging from plaice and dabs to the exceptional-tasting turbot. The subtle differences between the various flatfish are notoriously difficult to spot; some of them are even capable of hybridising. Good fish ID is a must if you want to be really sure that you've just caught a brill or a megrim.

Cod

Once the mainstay of the nation's fish and chip habit, cod are not as common as they used to be. While bass are the star of the summer fishing agenda, for those hardy souls willing to go out in cold winter weather cod are most often the target species. Cod tend to feed more by smell than sight and, as a result, large static baits are usually the order of the day. Lug worms, in one form or another, take a lot of beating. Several worms, the bigger the better, on a decent-sized hook (or better still a pennel rig where two hooks are used one above the other) are a good starting point for a cod session.

This cod fell to lug worm bait.

Bream

One of my favourite fish to eat, bream (most noticeably the black bream) tend to be a summer visitor to our shores. Bream move into the south coast in large numbers in the late spring.

Black bream are voracious feeders and their rat-a-tat bite is unmistakable. Photo: Mark Crame.

Black bream require a light tackle approach: a small hook holding a slither of squid is a popular bait and a whole squid head tends to sort out some of the better fish. A circle hook in a size 2 is about right, and a long flowing trace seems to give the best results. When I first fished the Channel Islands the charter skipper had great success with bream on feathers, tipping off each feather with a strip of squid. I've since used this method with great success around both Poole and Swanage, so it's definitely worth a try.

You might also be lucky enough to have a go at other members of this family, most notably the hard-fighting gilt-head bream which can be found in the creeks and estuaries around Cornwall in the summer months.

Sharks

There are many members of the shark family which you are likely to encounter afloat. Don't panic, however, since most of them are quite small. The bait-robbing lesser-spotted dogfish is much maligned, but sometimes it can be the only fish around prepared to take a bait. Dogfish will eat anything, but a fish bait tends to work best if you want to target them and their rather more interesting and sporting cousins, spurdogs and bull huss. (If you fancy a chance of a spurdog, head to Loch Etive in Scotland which is also an amazingly attractive place for a paddle.) Smooth-hounds are another member of the shark family which you might encounter, but they usually prefer a crab bait.

Huss and dogfish are generic names for various species of small shark.

The larger sharks that can sometimes be found in our waters are also sometimes targeted from a kayak. Indeed, I've spent the odd day off the north Devon coast in the company of anglers targeting large sharks with a whole mackerel out under a balloon. This kind of fishing is best left to the experts, however. I for one wouldn't fancy being in a kayak in close proximity to an angry porbeagle.

Tope

Tope are great fun to catch from a kayak. Tope will take a fish bait, usually right on the bottom. Whole mackerel or a bluey (a type of bait fish available from fishing tackle shops) will make a nice snack for a tope. The same bait is also likely to be pestered by dogfish, so it pays to think about taking a fair amount of bait out with you if you are targeting tope.

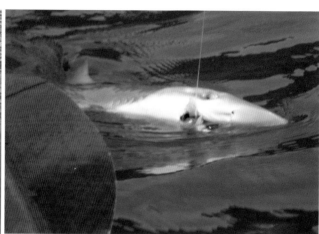

Tope have soft underbellies which can be bruised by rough hanlding over your knees or the deck of a boat. It's better for the fish if you can bring it, exhausted, alongside the boat and unhook it in the water.

Tope have a great set of teeth and also quite a rough skin so the use of a strong trace is in order. Some anglers will also use a rubbing leader, which is a section of stronger line attached between the main reel line and the trace so that the fish doesn't rub through the line.

Rays

A member of the shark family, rays look more like flatfish. Probably the easiest one to catch is the thornback ray, which is rather confusingly often referred to as skate. These are a very different beast from the 100lb (or more) real skate that you can catch in Scotland. Thornbacks tend to be present all year round further south, although they are more of a summer species in the north.

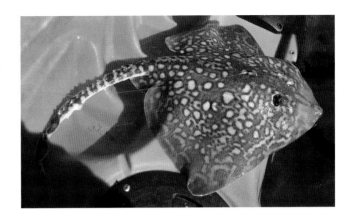

Thornback ray.
Photo: David Morris
www.anglersafloat.com

When you look at the ray's body shape, you can see how it feeds. It swims along the seabed and then settles down on its prey for lunch. This gives us a couple of bits of information. The first is not to strike too early, as it's very easy to pull the bait away when the ray has just settled on it but hasn't actually eaten it. The second is to use long-shanked strong hooks, as shorter patterns can lead to fish hooking themselves very deeply and being difficult to release successfully. I'd also use a relatively large hook for the same reason. Another advantage of a larger hook is that you don't have to put your fingers into the fish's mouth, which isn't a bright thing to do given the thornback's dental arrangements. Thornback rays can be caught on almost any bait while spotted, blond and small eyes tend to fall more often to fish baits (sandeels in particular).

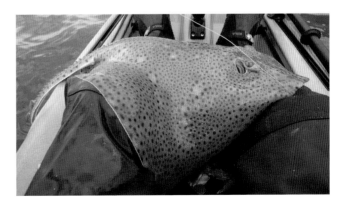

This fine blond ray was caught
off the north Devon coast.

FRESHWATER FISHING

*Membership of the British
Canoe Union includes a British
Waterways licence to paddle
on a number of UK waterways
including many canals.*

There is no reason why your kayak fishing should be limited to the sea, as a kayak gives you access to swims not normally reached by the bank-based angler. If you intend to coarse fish in the UK then you need an Environment Agency rod licence, available online or at post offices. You should also be aware that most English rivers and many canals have a closed season from 15th March to 15th June. To make things even more complicated, you also need permission, and often a licence, from the local angling club or landowner to fish from a boat. A few stretches of water are free to fish, but it's important to investigate beforehand who owns the fishing rights.

When it comes to the fishing itself, of the static methods, float fishing tends to work best as the kayak moves around a bit, and this makes techniques such as ledgering difficult. If you do want to stop the kayak moving, then tying up to the bank works well. Alternatively, do as the Americans do and take a couple of long bamboo poles with you. Drive these down through your scupper holes into the river bed.

While you can use the whole spectrum of fresh water fishing tactics from a kayak, most people that I know who fish in fresh water tend to use lures and to fish for predators, as this is the type of fishing at which the kayak excels.

Pike

Probably the top freshwater quarry from a kayak is the pike. Pike are the main freshwater predator, and lures are a very good way to fish for them. Trolling a lure behind the kayak can be a superb way to explore a river or canal. Pike will also take small silver fish either dead or alive, and trolling a small deadbait behind the kayak can work exceptionally well, a variation of the bank angler's tactic of 'wobbling'. Deadbaits can also be suspended below a decent sized float, and watching one of these go under as a large pike snaffles a deadbait can be excellent fun, a wide range of frozen pike baits are available from tackle shops, and it's worth asking what is working on your local waters.

A magnificent pike.
Photo: David Morris
www.anglersafloat.com

If you go bass fishing from the kayak at sea then the chances are that you've already got some gear which can be pressed into action for pike fishing as pike tackle is very similar to that used for bass fishing. When using lures for pike, which should all be returned to the water unharmed, it's best to use barbless hooks; trebles used to mount small fish should also be barbless. Pike are actually quite sensitive to rough handling so, for this reason, try to unhook them in the water. If you do have to bring them aboard, take an unhooking mat with you.

A voracious perch, caught on a Rapala CD9 Magnum lure.
Photo: Mark Crame

Other predators

It's not only the pike that you can catch with lures on rivers and still waters; there are also three other predators out there that can be targeted by anglers, namely the chub, perch and zander. The first two are very widely distributed, while the zander will take a bit more research to find a likely spot. Perch in particular are always likely to have a go at a lure, and are also quite easily caught on almost any common coarse fishing bait, although garden worms tend to catch the slightly bigger ones. Probably the best advice when fishing for predators is to try and think like a fish; these guys generally tend to be ambush predators, and pick a likely spot, with decent cover, where they can hide and then nip out and eat any passing victim. Look out for areas such as overhanging trees or bushes, variations in the bottom such as deep pools, thick weed beds, all these types of features will form a hiding place and are well worth exploring with a lure. The great advantage of using a kayak for freshwater lure fishing is that you can cover a really good amount of water and also get to present a lure in places that might be impossible to reach from the banks.

TAKING IT FURTHER

Travelling with your kayak fishing can take you to some extraordinary places, like fishing for cod in Sweden.
Photo: emotionkayaks.com

Once you've got the hang of fishing with your mates in sheltered coastal and inland waters, you may decide that the time has come to take it a little further. Extreme kayak fishing is a beyond the scope of this book, but there are a few things you can do to push the limits while remaining safe (you might even catch a few fish along the way).

Night fishing

Most shore fishing nowadays is done at night, and there is no reason not to go afloat at night in your kayak providing you've done a little homework first and planned for the trip.

The first thing you are going to need is a light, not just so you can see what you are doing but also so that other sea users can see you. If you are anchored up at night without a light you'll be invisible to other boat users and it won't be long before someone comes along and runs you over.

The light you are going to need is an all-round white light, the legal requirement being that it must be visible from every direction. In practical terms what this means is that it must be mounted on

This Scotty light mast can be attached to the deck using any of the Scotty mountings. Photo: scotty.com

some sort of mast which extends above your head so that it can always been seen and won't be blocked out by your body.

A number of companies make such a light, often with a suction base. Be aware that sometimes this kind of base won't stick very well to the surface of a plastic kayak hull. Some anglers use a different type of light where the batteries and controls are included inside the mast itself, and the mast is then clamped or cable tied to the angler's crate. This type comes highly recommended.

Another way to make your kayak more visible at night is to use SOLAS tape. Shore anglers will have seen something similar in the tape that is often wrapped around rod tips so they show up in the dark. The SOLAS certification also means you are getting a proper marine-grade tape. Use lengths of the tape down both sides of your kayak, and you'll be amazed how well it will show up with even the smallest amount of light. Try taking a picture at night using a flash to see how effective this type of tape can be. I know it sounds a bit over the top, but I've also put a couple of strips of SOLAS down the bottom of my kayak. If for any reason my kayak is upturned at night it will be easy for the rescue services to spot.

SOLAS reflective tape sticks
well to gelcoat or plastic.

Wreck fishing

As you gain experience, you may want to wander further a-field for your fishing. Wreck fishing can be great fun and very productive. Although some wrecks can be found very close to the coast, some require a little more effort to get to. Some wrecks are marked on charts, and this is a good place to start. Diving websites are another good source of information. The usual rules apply: build up to long paddles gradually and try to find someone else to go with you. Your fishing buddy should preferably be someone who has fished there before and knows the conditions. Always tell someone where you are going and when you plan to return.

Kayak sailing

You may have seen kayaks with sails on them. A sail can really extend the range of a kayak, and there are a number of designs available. Sailing rigs range from those used on Hobies, (kayaks designed with sailing in mind), to aftermarket bolt-on rigs that can be added to a wide range of kayaks. All can be great fun, but try them out with someone who knows what they are doing. In addition, don't rely on the sail to get you home as wind direction and force can change unexpectedly.

This Ultra is fitted with a Pacific Action sailing rig.

Look after the planet

Leave no trace

The fact that you've chosen to fish from a kayak is a boost to your green credentials; after all, it's far better to use a little muscle power rather than petrol or diesel to get to your favourite fishing spot. However, it's a harsh fact that anglers can include some of the worst litterers. I'm still deeply troubled by the sight of an angler on Westward Ho! rocks. He left a vast pile of plastic and line close to the water's edge and simply headed off to the nearest pub, obviously thinking that the ocean is a dustbin. A friend and I went over and cleaned up after him.

Often you find stuff on the beach that just shouldn't be there, litter which can last for centuries. People should want to take stuff home instead of polluting the planet, and not just to avoid negative press for anglers! Think about what you take afloat. Make sure that you bring any rubbish back with you and dispose of it safely. Cut up any waste line into small sections so it can't cause tangles at the landfill site.

One of the great benefits of kayak fishing is the ability to venture to secluded coves and even camp out at inaccessible places. Please leave everything as you found it; the sea is happy to wash away your footprints – make them the only trace you leave behind.

Sustainable fishing

The above naturally leads me onto the thorny subject of catch and release. With coarse fishing, catch and release is the norm; very few anglers would even consider tucking into a nice fresh carp. With game fishing the lines are blurred. Fresh water coarse and game fishing tend to be in more managed environments than the sea, however, which is where nearly all our eating fish come from.

Now I like eating fish as much as the next man (possibly even more) but the sea is not an inexhaustible resource. Over the course of this century, the industrialisation of fishing has had a major impact on the number and variety of fish available to the average angler. If you want to see just how much times have changed and how overfishing can affect fish stocks, then I highly recommend *Cod: A Biography of the Fish That Changed the World* by Mark Kurlansky.

Since Neanderthal times man has fished to feed himself, and there are those who insist on the right to take fish home. Nowadays, however, it is widely accepted that the sea is not jam-packed full of fish in the way it was before commercial fishing. Several of the species you are likely to encounter on your kayak are certainly a lot less common than they used to be. Rod and line fishing can have an effect on certain populations, breeding grounds or species.

My thoughts on the matter are: By all means take the occasional fish for your own consumption. Fresh caught fish is one of life's great pleasures, but think about how many fish you actually need.

Measuring up. Photo:
wildernesssystems.com

If you are intending to take fish home and eat them then it's worth noting that very small fish, often referred to as undersize, are protected by law. I've already covered the subject of minimum sizes for bass. DEFRA issues a list of minimum landing sizes, aimed at commercial fishermen, which is well worth looking up. For recreational fishermen, there is the old National Federation of Sea Anglers (NFSA) species list, which can now be found on the Angling Trust website. These sizes are more conservation minded and were used a lot by match fishermen. However, even fishing matches these days tend to be catch and release, so as to minimise any depletion of fish stocks.

Spread the word

To me, one of the most enjoyable aspects of kayak fishing is the newness of the whole thing. It's only been around for a few years in this country, and nearly everyone I have met in this new sport has been friendly and eager to help others start. On an Anglers Afloat training day I attended in September 2009, the instructor sadly announced that it was to be the last such day that the course could run. The dreaded health and safety concerns had made running any more of these free events too risky. He finished the last course by asking anyone who had been on that course (and indeed, any of the 200 or so anglers that he had trained) to do as much as possible to encourage newcomers to the sport. I thoroughly applaud these sentiments, and hope that this book has helped in some way to get you out and about on a kayak and catching fish.

I urge you to pass it on wherever possible. Let's try to keep this as the most amazingly friendly sport and help out newcomers in the same way that I was welcomed. Stay safe and, above all, know your limits. Fish within them and have fun.

INDEX

Go further, faster, and safer.

If you already paddle a sit on top kayak, you're bound to have wondered about sea kayaks. What's the big deal? you ask yourself. You sit inside and wear a spray deck but surely that's about it. Not much different to paddling a sit on top kayak really is it?

The reality is that although the skills required to paddle both kind of boats are similar, a sea kayak is a world apart. A far more seaworthy and efficient craft a sea kayak allows you to travel further, carrying much more gear, with less effort. Making for bigger, more enjoyable adventures in harder to reach places. So if you enjoy your sit on top, why not think about joining us on one of our sea kayak courses, holidays or expeditions and give yourself a chance to improve your paddling, navigation and safety skills whilst gaining first hand experience of how it feels to paddle a sea kayak. By the end of the course you will know if a sea kayak is for you and if it's not, you'll be a much more confident, knowledgeable and safer, sit on top paddler.

For a 72-page brochure e-mail us on brochure@pyb.co.uk now.

PLAS Y BRENIN
Canolfan Fynydd Genedlaethol • The National Mountain Centre
www.pyb.co.uk

Plas y Brenin Capel Curig Conwy LL24 OET Tel: 01690 720214 www.pyb.co.uk Email: info@pyb.co.uk